STRONGER THAN FEAR

A TRUE STORY FROM A LONE SOLDIER

DANIEL MANTICOF

Stronger Than Fear

Copyright © 2025 by Daniel Manticof

All rights reserved.

Published by Red Penguin Books

Bellerose Village, New York

ISBN

Digital 978-1-63777-819-7

Print 978-1-63777-820-3 | 978-1-63777-821-0

Certain names, places, and identifying details have been changed to protect the privacy of individuals and comply with censorship guidelines. The events described are based on true experiences.

No part of this book may be reproduced in any form or by any electronic or mechanical means, including information storage and retrieval systems, without written permission from the author, except for the use of brief quotations in a book review.

"He who has a why to live, can bear almost any how."

- FRIEDRICH NIETZSCHE

CONTENTS

Introduction	vii
Prologue	1
1. Roots Rediscovered	3
2. Returning to Argentina	8
3. A Journey of Discovery	14
4. Building the Foundation	21
5. Trials of Determination	26
6. Finding Strength in Support	32
7. A New Chapter in Combat	39
8. Remembering Nathanel Young Z"L	45
9. A Heavy Weight	48
10. The Calm Before the Storm	53

PART ONE
THE JOURNAL

The Entrance	63
Survival in the Sand	67
Finding Light in the Darkness	71
Under the Cover	73
The Meaning of Appreciation	77
A Glimpse of Comfort	81
A New Mission	85
David and the Drone	89
The Ground Beneath Us	95

PART TWO
THE JOURNAL

Searching the Shadows	103
Shabbat	107
The Questions of War	109
The Chaotic Night	113
The Capture	117
Storms and Elite Soldiers	121
The Sandwich	125

PART THREE
THE JOURNAL

First Ones In, Last Ones Out	133
The Light at the End of the Tunnel	137
Fire and Rain	141
Rocket Launcher	145
Conversations and Searches	149
Whispers of Hope	151
The Clearing Mission	153
A Test of Restraint	157
Faith in the Darkness	161
A Song in the Silence	165
11. The Road Back to Israel	167
12. Unmasking the Present	171
13. From the Front Lines to a New Fight	176
14. To the Next Lone Soldier	182
Closing Words	185
Acknowledgments	187

INTRODUCTION

Life has a way of taking unexpected turns, and my journey is no exception. I was born on June 23, 2001, in Argentina, during one of the most unstable periods in the country's modern history. In late 2001, Argentina faced one of the worst economic crises the nation had ever seen. Years of mounting debt, government overspending, and a fixed exchange rate system that could no longer hold, eventually pushed the economy to collapse. The government defaulted on more than $100 billion in debt—the largest sovereign default at the time. Banks froze citizens' savings accounts, known as the "corralito," and suddenly, people couldn't access their own money. The peso lost its value almost overnight. Inflation soared, and within weeks, the streets of Buenos Aires filled with protests, looting, and political chaos. Five presidents came and went in less than two weeks.

The on-ground reality was harsh. Middle-class families were thrown into poverty. Businesses closed, jobs vanished, and neighborhoods that once thrived fell into silence. My parents, like many others, were left with an impossible choice: stay and hope things got better, or leave behind everything they knew to try and build a new life somewhere else.

They chose to leave.

My parents had built their lives during what they hoped would be a stable future, but the crisis hit hard and fast. They were working for the ousted government and found themselves on the wrong side of a system that had imploded. Their jobs vanished, the peso crashed, and the uncertainty was unbearable. With no money, no stability, and no clear path forward, they left everything behind—family, friends, and the only home they had ever known—in search of a safer life.

And so, when I was just eight months old, we boarded a plane to the United States. My parents didn't speak English and carried only what they could fit into a few suitcases. We landed in New Jersey, not just as immigrants but as survivors of a crumbling system, holding on to nothing but faith and the hope of starting over. They had no roadmap—only the determination to rebuild from scratch in a country with a completely different language, culture, and way of life.

Growing up in the United States, our family built a new life from scratch. Eleven of us gathered every Friday night around the Shabbat table, our traditions grounding us in a world that felt foreign. My parents, having lost everything in Argentina, taught us resilience, faith, and the importance of community.

As the years passed, my parents did everything they could to build stability. But for some reason, I always felt a strange disconnect. Unlike my siblings, who seemed to adjust more easily, I carried a quiet restlessness. Maybe it was because I had left Argentina too young to remember it, but just old enough to feel the absence. I couldn't shake the feeling that something about my identity was incomplete. I was grateful for everything my parents had given us, but deep down, I needed to understand where I truly came from.

That's when the opportunity came to return to Argentina—to visit the place I had only heard about in family stories, and more importantly, to spend time with my grandmother. I had only known her through video calls and the faded photos on my parents' shelves. She was a striking young woman in the pictures—sharp features, proud posture—but when I finally saw her in person, she was much older, frailer. Her eyes, though, still carried a strength and a sadness I could not name. There was a quiet pain in them, like someone who had seen a lot but spoken very little of it.

In many ways, meeting her was like meeting a part of myself that I hadn't known was missing.

From a young age, I attended a Jewish private school in New Jersey, where I learned early on about Israel's history—the wars, the terrorist attacks, and the enduring spirit of our people. Those stories stayed with me. I always felt a pull to protect, even if I didn't yet understand why.

Years later, that pull turned into action. I left behind everything familiar to enlist in the IDF as a lone soldier. It wasn't easy—a new country, a new language, no family nearby. But in those moments, I discovered something extraordinary: the strength of the people of Israel. The unwavering support we received—strangers offering meals, families opening their homes, communities standing behind us—reminded me that I was never truly alone. Their kindness became a lifeline, giving me the will to adapt and move forward, even when it felt impossible.

This book isn't just about war. It's about what happens to the human spirit when faced with the unimaginable. It's about love, faith, and the unbreakable bonds that keep us moving forward, even when the world seems to crumble around us. It's about the unbreakable spirit of a lone soldier—and the extraordinary unity of a nation that refuses to let anyone stand alone.

Writing this book has been both a healing process and a responsibility. I made a promise to myself when I carried that pocket-sized journal into Gaza that if I made it out alive, I'd tell my story so others could understand not just what we endured, but why we endured it.

PROLOGUE
CROSSING THE BORDER

The border loomed ahead of us in the early morning darkness, an invisible line separating familiarity from the unknown. October 30, 2023, wasn't just another day—it was the moment everything we had trained for became real. The air was thick, almost suffocating, as if it carried the weight of the battles waiting for us across the fence. The silence among us was heavy, broken only by the distant sounds of explosions. At 03:30, we crossed into Gaza. The world beyond the border was chaos. Explosions erupted around us, their flashes momentarily lighting up the shattered terrain. The ground trembled underfoot with every nearby impact, and the deafening roar of tank fire filled the air. My heart raced as I gripped my machine gun, my mind alert to every noise, every shadow. Before we entered, our *Mefaked Pluga*—our high-ranking company commander—gathered us close. His voice was steady, his words deliberate: "Our mission is to bring the hostages back to their families and to protect one another. We are soldiers of the IDF. We will not enter Gaza the way Hamas entered Israel. We will act with precision, honor, and purpose."

His words cut through the noise of fear and uncertainty. This wasn't about revenge—it was about showing restraint in a place that had seen too much blood.

Then, before moving out, we recited the *Shema Yisrael,* one of the most sacred prayers in Judaism—a declaration of faith, unity, and remembrance. For generations, Jews have recited it in moments of danger and hope. Saying it together, in that moment, was more than tradition. It gave us a sense of protection and of shared purpose. It reminded us who we were and why we were there.

The terrain grew increasingly hostile the deeper we moved into Gaza. Every step felt heavier, not just from the weight of my gear but from the tension that gripped us all. Suddenly, we spotted small buildings still standing amidst the ruins. One of the commanders at the front halted the formation. A flashlight beam flickered inside one of the structures, and before we could process it, the sound of gunfire erupted. The chaos was instant. My platoon commander shouted an order for me to cover a specific direction. Positioned at the very back of the formation, I swung my machine gun around, scanning for any signs of movement behind us. My role as the gunner meant I had to protect the unit's rear—a responsibility that felt heavier in moments like this. The tanks with us reacted quickly. Two terrorists were identified and eliminated before they could pose a greater threat. The flashlights disappeared, and the gunfire stopped, but the tension lingered. We regrouped, checked for injuries, and pressed on.

Amidst the chaos, I found myself thinking about the path that had led me here–the decisions, the sacrifices, all those moments that shaped my journey. From my early days growing up in New Jersey as one of nine children, to the choice of leaving everything behind and enlisting as a lone soldier in Israel, every step seemed to lead to this one.

This is where my story begins.

CHAPTER 1
ROOTS REDISCOVERED

Growing up in New Jersey, my life was defined by two things: the constant energy of a big family and the drive to carve out my own path in a world that often felt overwhelming. Chaos was the norm in our family of eleven. The house was always alive with noise, laughter, arguments, and the shuffle of countless shoes as my brothers and sisters rushed in and out. Yet, even in the whirlwind of our daily lives, there were moments of stillness, giving a place for meaning to settle in our busy lives. Every Friday night, as the chaos of the week gave way to the peace of Shabbat, we gathered around the table. Those dinners were sacred—not just for the food, but because they brought us together, no matter what. They taught me that unity gives strength, and that even in chaos, family is where resilience begins.

DISCOVERING MY STRENGTHS

As a kid, I was restless, always looking for ways to challenge myself. Whether it was climbing trees in the backyard or chasing after a soccer ball with my brothers, I was drawn to movement and competition. In school, I struggled at first, especially with English. The language didn't come naturally to me, and I often felt like I was playing catch-up. At home, my parents spoke to me in Spanish almost all the time. It was the language of comfort, discipline, love, and tradition. But my brothers and sisters—who spent most of their days in American classrooms—

would come back speaking in fast, fluent English. Over time, our house developed its own rhythm, a "Spanglish" dynamic that only made sense to us. Sentences would start in one language and end in another. "¿Puedes pass me the remote?" or "Mom, él dijo que I can't go," were normal ways of speaking. It was messy, hilarious, and ours. But instead of letting the challenge of English discourage me, it lit a fire inside me. I worked harder, stayed later, and pushed myself to improve. Slowly but surely, I began to find my footing, building confidence in both languages and embracing the cultural richness that came with being bilingual. By the time I reached high school, that determination had become part of who I was. I threw myself into sports, finding in them a sense of purpose and belonging.

LESSONS FROM THE FIELD

Wrestling was my first introduction to discipline at age 15. On the mat, there was no room for excuses—it was just you and your opponent. Every practice, every match, pushed me to my limits. It was exhausting, but it taught me how to persevere, even when every muscle in my body was screaming at me to stop. Soccer, though, was where I truly came alive. There was something magical about the game—the way it brought people together, the way it demanded both skill and strategy. By my senior year, I had earned the title of captain.

As captain, I wasn't just leading a team—I was learning how to lead people, how to motivate them, and bring out their best. One game stands out in my memory. We were down by two goals at halftime, and everyone looked defeated. I stood in the middle of the locker room and reminded them why we played—not for the score, but for each other. We came back onto the field with renewed energy, and though we didn't win that game, we left everything we had out there. Those moments on the field taught me lessons I didn't fully appreciate at the time: the value of teamwork, the strength that comes from unity, and the importance of giving your all, even when the odds aren't in your favor.

THE PANDEMIC YEARS

Like most high school seniors, I had imagined my graduation day for years. I pictured the traditional ceremony: walking across the stage in a cap and gown, hearing my name over the loudspeaker, the sound of applause, and seeing my family in the crowd; smiling, proud, maybe even tearing up a little. For my parents, especially after all the sacrifices they made coming to the U.S., it was supposed to be a moment of arrival. A moment that said, *we made it.*

But 2020 had other plans.

When the pandemic shut everything down, our school canceled the in-person graduation ceremony. No crowds. No handshakes. No photos with classmates in the gym. I remember getting the email and just staring at it. My stomach dropped. It wasn't dramatic, just quiet disappointment that stuck with me. At first, I didn't even want to talk about it. But later that week, I called a few friends. We were all feeling the same—like something had been stolen from us without warning. We had done the work, but the celebration disappeared.

It was my mom who came up with the idea for a ceremony at home. She said, "You worked hard, and we're going to honor that, even if it's just us." At first, I resisted. It felt small, almost like pretending. But when the day came, she decorated the living room, played the graduation march on a speaker, and handed me a rolled-up piece of paper with my name on it. My siblings clapped. We took pictures in the backyard.

It wasn't what I expected—but in some ways, it meant more. The effort my family put in reminded me that recognition doesn't have to be big to be meaningful. That day grounded me in a new way. It was a quiet yet powerful reminder that sometimes, even when the world shifts, your people show up, and that's what matters most.

THE PULL OF ARGENTINA

As the world slowed down, my thoughts began drifting to a place I had never truly known: Argentina. My parents spoke about it often—sometimes with warmth, other times with a heaviness they didn't always explain. They talked about their old neighborhood, about the small bakery around the corner from my grandmother's house, about the sound of fútbol games echoing through the streets on Sunday afternoons. Over time, those stories painted a picture in my mind that felt unfinished. I realized I didn't just want to hear about Argentina anymore; I wanted to see it for myself.

At first, I brought it up casually during dinner. But the more I spoke, the more serious the conversations became. My parents were surprised by how strongly I felt, but also supportive. I think they sensed it was more than a vacation to me—it was something I needed to do. I wanted to walk through the city of Buenos Aires and see the neighborhood where my parents grew up. I wanted to eat *empanadas* in a busy plaza, to hear the music, and to understand the rhythm of a place that had shaped my family in ways I was only beginning to understand.

Buenos Aires is one of the most vibrant cities in Latin America, often called the "Paris of the South" for its wide boulevards, elegant architecture, and deep cultural roots. But, it's also a city marked by hardship—especially during the 2001 economic crisis that forced my parents to leave. That collapse didn't just impact bank accounts; it shattered trust, upended families, and left scars that were hard to erase.

A JOURNEY INTO THE UNKNOWN

At the time, I thought the trip would be simple: two months to reconnect with family, explore the country, and satisfy my curiosity. But as I packed my bags and prepared for the journey, I couldn't shake the feeling that this was the beginning of something much bigger. I was leaving behind the world I had always known, the familiar streets of New Jersey, the routines of high school, the comfort of my family, for a country I had only heard about in stories.

The morning of my flight, I sat quietly by the window, watching the sun rise over my neighborhood one last time. My bag was heavy, not just with clothes but with questions, hopes, and a sense of purpose I couldn't quite articulate. At the airport, surrounded by strangers rushing to their own destinations, I felt the first pangs of doubt. What if Argentina wasn't what I expected? What if I didn't belong there? But as the plane began to ascend, the doubt melted into a strange kind of calm. This was my chance to find answers, to explore a side of myself I had only ever heard about in stories told at family dinners. I stared out the window as the ground disappeared beneath the clouds, carrying me toward the unknown.

By the time the plane touched down in Buenos Aires, I felt a strange mix of excitement and nervousness. I was stepping into a world that was both foreign and familiar, a place where my past and future would collide in ways I couldn't yet comprehend. Little did I know, this journey would stretch far beyond the borders of Argentina and lead me to discoveries that would shape the rest of my life.

CHAPTER 2
RETURNING TO ARGENTINA

I was nineteen years old when I stepped off the plane in Buenos Aires in April 2021. The air hit me immediately—humid, warm, and full of energy. Inside the airport, the sound of rapid Spanish echoed all around me. I understood most of it, but speaking it again after so long felt unfamiliar.

Outside, the city buzzed with life. Buses and cars weaved through traffic, horns blaring in what felt like a language of their own. Street vendors called out, offering choripán (a chorizo sandwich) and dulce de leche (a sweet caramel spread) from small carts parked along the sidewalks. The smell of grilled meats, fresh pastries, and gasoline all mixed in the air—overwhelming, but in the best way.

As I drove through the streets, I noticed the layers of Buenos Aires. Colonial buildings with peeling paint stood beside trendy cafés and busy supermarkets. Murals of famous figures like Evita and Maradona covered old brick walls—like history was wailing instead of whispering. It was loud, messy, and beautiful.

Compared to my hometown in New Jersey, where things were orderly and quiet, Buenos Aires felt alive and unfiltered. In Jersey, I was used to schedules and routines. Here, everything seemed to flow more freely; there was a natural rhythm in the chaos.

Even before I reached my destination, I knew this trip would be different. Argentina didn't just feel like the country where I was born. It felt like something I needed to rediscover: one street, one sound, one smell at a time.

A REUNION ETCHED IN TIME

When I first visited my grandmother, Sara, at the nursing home, the moment felt like something I would carry with me forever. We hadn't seen each other in years, but the connection was instant. As I approached, her eyes widened and her smile lit up the room. She reached out and we hugged tightly—as if trying to make up for all the years and distance in one embrace.

"Mi amor, estás en casa," she said softly. *My love, you're home.*

Even though she smiled, I noticed how her body moved more slowly, carefully. At 82, time had left its marks, but her warmth and wit were still sharp. That first afternoon, we sat together in the small courtyard outside her room, drinking *mate*, a traditional Argentine herbal tea, and catching up.. I couldn't stop looking at her—studying the lines on her face, the way her hands shook slightly as she poured water, the way she laughed at things only grandmothers find funny.

It wasn't long before the real reason for her tiredness became clear. Just days before my arrival, doctors had recommended open-heart surgery due to worsening heart problems. Without it, they warned, she might have only a few months to live.

But my grandmother, in true Sara fashion, refused.

"I'd rather live my life fully for a few months," she said, "than spend it tied to a hospital bed with wires and medicine." Her words were calm, almost peaceful—but they hit me hard. I tried to reason with her, to convince her that maybe the surgery would give her more time. But deep down, I knew there was no changing her mind. She had always chosen dignity and strength over fear.

A NEW ROLE

My planned two-month stay stretched into something I never saw coming. One evening, I was sitting at a small café near the nursing home when my mom called from New Jersey. Her voice was calm, but I could tell it wasn't easy.

"We can't come right now," she said gently. "But we need you to stay. Abuela needs help, and there's no one else."

That was it. No dramatic breakdown, no big speech—just a quiet moment that flipped my entire life upside down.

At first, I didn't know what the hell I was doing. I had no long-term plan, no idea how long I'd be in Argentina, no roadmap. I was 19, and suddenly I had to grow up fast. I needed to figure out how to live like an adult—in a country I hadn't really known since I was a baby.

The first real challenge I faced was finding a place to live. I considered staying close to the nursing home, but I decided to rent a small, bare apartment just a few blocks away. It was the first time I had ever lived completely on my own. I was juggling the role of caregiver, student, and young adult, figuring out how to be independent.

Thankfully, cooking wasn't something I had to learn from scratch. Growing up, I had often helped my mom in the kitchen. Just by watching and assisting, I'd picked up how to prepare soups, empanadas, chicken, and other simple meals. That experience made the adjustment smoother. I actually found comfort in cooking. It gave me a sense of home, even in this unfamiliar city.

Then came the decision about what to do with my time. I couldn't just sit around. I wanted to work and study—but how? I barely knew the local system. I started researching online and asking cousins for advice. That's when I realized something important: I spoke fluent English in a country where most people didn't. It gave me a real advantage—especially for companies dealing with international clients or looking to expand beyond Spanish-speaking markets.

That's how I landed a job as a sales representative at a solar energy company. It wasn't glamorous, but it gave me a paycheck and helped me learn how to interact professionally. It also kept me busy, which helped me feel like I had some control over the chaos.

At the same time, I enrolled at UADE (Universidad Argentina de la Empresa), studying Global Business Management. My schedule was full: classes during the day, work in the afternoons, and visits to my grandmother in between. I was always tired, always moving, but little by little, I started to adapt.

A DECISION TO LIVE FULLY

Despite her declining health, my grandmother's humor and spirit never faded. She found joy in the smallest things—especially during our walks to the nearby café. I would hold her hand as we strolled slowly from the nursing home, feeling the warmth and weight of her fingers in mine. People passing by might have seen just two figures walking down the street, but to me, each step was filled with memory, trust, and love.

Once we arrived at the café, I would order *medialunas* for her (a type of Argentinian pastry). And then, with a mischievous grin, she would sneak an extra pastry into her pocket when she thought I wasn't looking, fully aware she wasn't supposed to indulge because of her health. "Just one more," she'd whisper, dipping it into her coffee as if it were her last great indulgence—a small act of joy and defiance that made me laugh and love her even more.

Her decision to forgo surgery was always on my mind, but watching her find happiness in those little moments softened my worry. She reminded me that life is often measured not by how long we live, but by how we live the time we're given.

One evening, as we sat quietly in the courtyard outside her room, a soft breeze moved through the trees. My grandmother turned to me and smiled.

"You remind me of him," she said softly, her eyes fixed on something far beyond the skyline. "Your smile ... the way you stay positive, even when things are hard. That was your grandfather."

I didn't say anything at first. I had barely known him—he passed away when I was just a young child, too young to form memories. But she carried him with her in every word, every glance, every story that hadn't yet been told.

"He used to come home after the longest, hardest days," she continued. "But no matter how tired he was, he walked through the door with a smile. That gave me strength. And now ... I see that in you."

Her voice was calm, but it landed like a wave. To be compared to someone she had loved so deeply—someone whose memory still lit up her face—meant more than I could explain.

A DIFFICULT GOODBYE

By January 2022, nine months after my arrival, time had quietly run out. One morning, as I finished a run at a nearby park, my phone buzzed. It was my Aunt Nancy, her voice tight with urgency: "Daniel, come to the nursing home now."

I jumped on a bike and pedaled as fast as I could, weaving through traffic as the city blurred around me. When I arrived, the look on the nurses' faces told me everything. My grandmother's breathing was shallow, her body still. My uncle stood beside her, head bowed, whispering a quiet apology.

Shabbat, the holy day of rest in Judaism, was approaching fast. It begins every Friday at sundown. In Jewish tradition, burials must take place before Shabbat begins, out of deep respect for the dead. That meant we had just a few hours to arrange everything.

The rush that followed didn't feel real. Phone calls, logistics, paperwork—it all blurred together. My mother, still in the U.S. and unable to fly in on time, joined the moment by video call. I held the phone carefully, trying to steady my hands so she could see the room—see her mother one last time. Her sobs came through the speaker, raw and uncontrollable.

I didn't know what to say. I wanted to comfort her, to say something—anything—that would make it hurt less. But the words stuck in my throat. My eyes were burning, my heart heavy. At that moment, we didn't need words. We were both grieving the same woman, one my mother had known for a lifetime, and one I had barely begun to know.

The burial was simple, raw. I helped lower the coffin with my uncle and a few close family members. My hands gripped the rope tightly as I watched the earth cover her. In that moment, I felt a wave of emptiness and gratitude—gratitude for her life, her stories, and the strength she had passed on to me.

CHAPTER 3
A JOURNEY OF DISCOVERY

After my grandmother passed away, I was left in a fog. Her absence created a silence that pushed me to reflect —not just on her life, but on mine. I felt unanchored, uncertain of what came next, and did not know whether to continue with business school. Somewhere in that uncertainty, I started thinking more deeply about identity, purpose, and where I truly belonged.

I'd grown up with a strong connection to the Jewish community. Stories, traditions, and Hebrew school had shaped my understanding of who I was. But now, I wanted to experience it more fully—to move beyond books and holidays and feel it in my bones. That's when I heard about Taglit Birthright, a ten-day, all-expenses-paid trip to Israel for Jewish young adults. The goal was to explore our heritage, connect with Israeli life, and maybe even find a deeper sense of belonging.

I applied. A few weeks later, I was accepted. I didn't know it then, but the trip would become a turning point in my life.

TOUCHING THE LAND

Israel didn't just look different, it felt different. The moment I stepped out of the airport, I was hit by a wave of heat and energy that never quite left me. Our group, made up of young Jews from all over the world, started our journey in Jerusalem—

a city layered with history and belief. Walking through its streets, I felt like I was stepping through time.

At the Western Wall, I stood quietly, hands pressed against ancient stones. I didn't cry or feel anything dramatic. But I did feel still, like I was finally standing in a place that had been calling me for a long time.

One of the heaviest stops on the trip was Yad Vashem, the Holocaust memorial and museum. I had learned about the Holocaust growing up, but this was different. Seeing the photos, reading the letters, hearing survivor testimonies-it hit me in a way textbooks never could. It gave me a clearer understanding of why Israel exists, and why protecting it matters so much.

After our visit to Yad Vashem, something stirred in me that I couldn't quite shake. Later that night, I called my dad. I told him how powerful the experience had been, how it made history feel more personal. That's when he shared something with me, something I had never heard before.

He told me that his family had been fleeing Ukraine during the war, trying to cross into Poland. It was a time when Jewish families across Eastern Europe were being hunted, cornered, and massacred—not just by the Nazis, but also by neighbors and militias who had been poisoned by antisemitic propaganda for generations.

His voice was steady, but the words cut deep. They were desperate, scared, holding on to hope. But as they crossed a bridge, they came face to face with Ukrainian soldiers. These weren't men following orders. They were drunk on hatred, filled with cruelty, and they wanted to kill Jews simply for the joy of it. Right there on that bridge, in front of his wife and children, they shot my great-grandfather in cold blood. No reason. No mercy. Just because he was a Jew.

The rest of the family ran, screaming, broken, surviving only by luck and the sheer will to live. They crossed into Poland with nothing but trauma and the weight of what they'd witnessed. That story hidden in the silence of our family was now mine to carry.

My father spoke in a calm voice, but I could hear the pain behind every word. It wasn't just a story, it was a wound, passed down through generations. I sat there in silence after the call, the image of that bridge burned into my mind. It was more than just a tale of loss; it was a reminder that hatred didn't need a reason. Sometimes it just waited for the right moment—and people—to let it loose.

That night, I realized something profound: I wasn't just standing in Israel as a curious visitor. I was standing here because they didn't get the chance. Because someone before me was murdered for being a Jew, and someone else had to run so I could one day stand free. That bridge in Ukraine, soaked in terror and loss, was part of my journey, too.

It became clear to me that I wasn't only exploring identity—I was reclaiming it. I wasn't just looking for who I was; I was continuing something others had died for. I was taking their silence, their pain, their memory, and turning it into something alive.

And that feeling, that awareness, began to reshape how I saw myself in the story of our people. I wasn't just a visitor. I was a descendant of survivors. A bearer of memory. A soldier in spirit, even before I put on the uniform.

THE UNEXPECTED INFLUENCE

One of the people who impacted me most wasn't a tripmate but our group's security guard, Feras. He was a Druze Arab, part of a small religious and ethnic community in Israel known for their deep loyalty to the state and their mandatory service in the IDF. Despite being ethnically Arab, the Druze community has a unique identity and a strong sense of duty toward Israel. Feras had served as a combat soldier, and between bus rides and security checks, he told me about his time in uniform.

His stories weren't heroic in the way action movies are. They were honest—about fear, responsibility, and loyalty to something greater than yourself. What struck me wasn't just what he did, but how much it meant to him. He spoke about honor, about protecting people, about unity in a country that was constantly on edge.

Hearing him talk made me pause. I had always looked up to soldiers, but Feras made me think differently. His pride and sense of purpose lit something inside me. I started asking myself harder questions: What was I doing with my life? What did I stand for? And if he, someone from a different background entirely, was so committed to this country, why wasn't I?

That's when the idea first took hold. The idea that I could come back—not just for another trip, but to give something. To serve. To protect. To make my presence here matter.

What began as a ten-day visit quickly became a crossroad to the future. I returned to Argentina with more questions than answers, but one thing was clear: my relationship with Israel had changed. It felt like something I needed to be part of—not from a distance, but from within.

FINDING A NEW PATH

When I returned to Argentina from Israel, something inside me had shifted. Even though I had only spent a short time there, I felt a strong pull to explore more. There was a sense that I had just scratched the surface, and I wanted more than a ten-day glimpse—I wanted a real opportunity to try out something that simply felt right for me. I began researching ways to return in a more meaningful way, and two programs stood out: the Masa Internship program and the Machal IDF Volunteer Program.

The Masa Internship program offered young adults the chance to live and work in Israel, gaining valuable experience in various fields while immersing themselves in the culture. The program provided internships in industries like technology, business, and education, along with benefits such as Hebrew language classes and cultural trips. It was appealing for its professional opportunities and the chance to build a global network.

But it was the Machal program that resonated more deeply. Machal, which means "Volunteers from Abroad," had a rich history. It began in 1948 when volunteers came to Israel during its war of independence, and it still allowed non-Israeli Jews to serve in the IDF. Participants trained like regular soldiers, learned Hebrew, and were placed in various units based on their skills. It was an opportunity to make a tangible contribution, to serve alongside Israeli soldiers and understand their experiences firsthand.

Of course, the idea of joining the military, especially a foreign one, was intimidating. I had plenty of worries. The language barrier was one of the biggest, and the thought of not fully understanding commands or instructions in high-stress situations was nerve-wracking. Then there was the physical challenge. I knew the IDF had high standards, and I questioned whether I could keep up, whether I could carry the weight, endure the drills, and hold my own beside guys who'd been preparing their whole lives for this.

But even with all those fears, something inside me kept pushing forward. I knew it wouldn't be easy, but I wasn't looking for easy. I was looking for something real—something that would stretch me and, hopefully, shape me into the person I was trying to become.

Both paths were appealing, so I applied to both, unsure which one would open first. Then, just a week later, an email arrived from the Ministry of Defense. My heart pounded as I read it: I had been accepted to start the drafting process for the IDF. Excitement and nerves battled inside me. I knew this was a serious commitment—one that would change everything.

When I told my parents, the reactions were immediate, but different. My mom was worried. Deep down, she understood my decision, but the thought of her son going into the army, especially so far from home, filled her with anxiety. My dad, on the other hand, nodded and said he believed that it would shape me into a strong man. He trusted my judgment and felt that this experience would teach me things no classroom ever could.

My siblings were understanding. They had grown up hearing the same stories I had—about Israel's history, the struggle for survival, and the pride that came with standing up for something meaningful. Still, it wasn't easy. As the older brother, I had always felt a quiet responsibility to be present, to guide and set an example. Part of me felt guilty for leaving them behind. But another part of me knew I had to follow what I felt in my gut—this deep pull to serve, to grow, and to become the person I believed I was meant to be.

My decision to serve wasn't just about a trip or a program. Deep down, it was also something much more personal. Growing up as one of nine children, I often felt like just another voice in the crowd—loved, yes, but easily overlooked. In a family so large and full of unique personalities and talents, I sometimes questioned what made me stand out. I wasn't the best at school, or the most athletic, or the loudest at the dinner table. And yet, there was always a quiet drive inside me, a need to prove that I mattered in my own way.

Part of me believed that if I did something truly meaningful—something brave and selfless—my parents would look at me differently. Not out of favoritism, but out of pride. I imagined my siblings, who were scattered across the country, hearing the news that I had joined the army and feeling something like admiration. Maybe even inspiration.

It wasn't about glory. It was about purpose. About becoming someone who didn't just blend into the family photo, but who took a step forward and said, *"This is who I am. This is what I believe in."*

I understood instinctively that serving in the IDF would be something that brought my entire family together emotionally, even if we were physically apart. I knew that this decision would make them proud—and perhaps more importantly, it would help me feel proud of myself.

CHAPTER 4
BUILDING THE FOUNDATION

After months of preparation, the day had finally come. I was on my way to Israel, my entire life packed into two suitcases and a backpack. As I boarded the plane, I felt a mix of anticipation and uncertainty. I knew I was about to face challenges that would test my resilience, patience, and strength. But the *unknowns* loomed just as large, making me wonder how prepared I truly was. Settling into my seat, the reality of leaving everything familiar behind began to sink in. It was a strange feeling to think that I'd be turning twenty-one during the flight, thousands of feet above the world, crossing borders and time zones. Just before midnight, a flight attendant handed me a small dessert, sparking a playful idea. I flipped the cupcake over, spread pudding on it like frosting, and added a piece of candy on top, making my own birthday cake. As I worked, I noticed a few curious glances, and someone nearby chuckled, asking for a slice. "It's my birthday," I explained, and they broke into a chorus of "Happy Birthday." This small gesture brought warmth to the moment and reminded me that even here, among strangers, I wasn't entirely alone.

When we landed, my aunt was waiting for me, and as we embraced, I felt some of my anxiety dissipate. She whisked me away to a restaurant where we celebrated my birthday. It was the perfect start to my journey, filling me with a sense of belonging and a readiness to face whatever lay ahead.

SETTLING IN AND MEETING MY COMMUNITY

The first few days were a whirlwind of adjusting and settling in. I quickly found myself surrounded by people who, like me, had come to Israel to connect with their roots and make a difference. Some were from the United States, others from Venezuela, Ethiopia, the Netherlands, and beyond. Despite our different backgrounds, we all shared the same goal: to understand and contribute to this country that meant so much to us.

One of the first people I really connected with was Ariel. I remember feeling overwhelmed by all the new faces and the fast-paced Hebrew flying around me. Then Ariel turned to me and, with a big grin, started speaking Spanish. Just like that, I felt like I could breathe again. I learned that he was from France, but his mother had always spoken to him in Spanish at home. We clicked immediately. It was a huge relief to have someone who understood both the language and the mix of emotions I was feeling. We both had our sights set on making it into a strong combat unit in the IDF. That shared ambition built a bond between us right from the start.

A few days after settling in, I joined a *Mechina*, a preparatory program designed to help new recruits and volunteers acclimate to Israeli life and the basics of military culture. The *Mechina* wasn't just a training ground; it was a place of connection. People from all walks of life came together with different reasons for being there, but a shared sense of purpose.

We spent our days learning the essentials: Israeli history, Hebrew, and military basics—but we also shared laughs, late-night talks, and the growing realization that we were becoming each other's support system. Hebrew, for most of us, wasn't easy. It's written from right to left, with a whole new alphabet and grammar structure that felt completely unfamiliar. For someone who didn't grow up speaking it, just reading a sentence could take effort. But day by day, it started to make more sense. Ariel and I often stayed up planning our goals, talking about where we wanted to serve, and pushing each other to stay focused. It helped having someone who understood both the language and the challenge. We reminded each other of why we came here—and how far we were willing to go to earn our place.

One of the best parts of the *Mechina* was the excursions across Israel. Together, we visited historical sites, wandered through ancient cities, and explored landscapes that felt as old as time. Each trip added a new layer to my understanding of the land—connecting the history I had read about to the soil I now stood on.

TRANSITIONING TO MICHVE ALON

After completing the Mechina (*meh-khee-NAH*, a pre-army preparatory program), it was time to move on to Michve Alon (*meekh-VEH ah-LOHN*), a training base that marked the next stage of my journey. This step was different. Here, we weren't just adjusting to life in Israel; we were becoming part of the military. The moment I was handed my dark green uniform, a sense of purpose washed over me. The fabric was heavier than I expected, both in weight and in meaning. Wearing it, I felt connected to the generations of soldiers who had defended this land before me.

Boarding the bus to Michve Alon was surreal. Everyone was dressed in the same uniform, sitting in silence, each person lost in their own thoughts. We knew we were stepping into something serious, something that would change us. When we arrived, we were ordered to line up immediately for our first briefing. This was the military now—a new world, with its own rules, its own language, and expectations. I realized that I'd need to adapt quickly if I was going to succeed. Training at Michve Alon was challenging. The emphasis on Hebrew grew stronger, with daily language classes that were both mentally and physically exhausting. Learning Hebrew was more than just understanding words; it was about fully integrating into the life and culture of Israel. We spent hours every day practicing, knowing that mastering the language was critical if we were to understand commands, communicate effectively, and truly be part of the team.

Even though the classes were demanding, we were fortunate to have teachers who were deeply committed to helping us succeed. They didn't just lecture from the front of the classroom—they sat beside us, walking us through lessons at a comfortable pace, ensuring that no one was left behind. Their patience and dedication made all the difference, creating an environment where even the most difficult concepts felt achievable. When I started those classes, I held onto a mindset that became my guiding principle: "Anyone wanting to learn will learn." That belief kept me motivated, even on the hardest days. I knew that if I put in the effort, I could learn the language faster and open the doors to a deeper connection with my surroundings and my unit. Every day was a step forward, and that mindset was what pushed me to keep going.

THE REALITY OF MILITARY TRAINING

Along with Hebrew lessons, we began learning the basics of military skills, including how to handle weapons. One of the pivotal moments was the day we practiced shooting for the first time. Nearly every soldier in Israel goes through this experience at least once, and the weight of the rifle in my hands reminded me of the responsibility I was taking on. It was sobering and a little intimidating, but each lesson brought me a growing confidence and pride in what I was learning. During training, our commanders pushed us to our limits, emphasizing discipline and teamwork. Some days were tougher than others. There were times I felt like giving up, wondering if I was really cut out for this. But whenever I felt the weight of self-doubt, I remembered why I was here—to connect with my heritage and contribute to a place that was becoming more than just a country; it was becoming a part of who I was.

Slowly, I started to feel a shift within myself. My surroundings were no longer strange; they had become familiar. The group of strangers I had once hesitated to approach had become my friends, people who understood my journey in a way no one else could. The landscapes we trained in, the long hours, and the shared challenges had built a foundation I could stand on.

CHAPTER 5
TRIALS OF DETERMINATION

As time passed, my Hebrew improved steadily. I grew more comfortable with the language, but I knew it wasn't quite enough for what lay ahead. My ambitions were high, and I was determined to push my limits. I had set my sights on something challenging: the special forces selection exams. I knew these exams would test me like nothing else.

The first trial I took on was the tryout for the paratroopers. Shortly after, I faced the infamous *Yom Sayarot*, or "Selection Day." This event was an intense, grueling tryout for some of the IDF's most elite units—teams that operate on land, sea, and air. Candidates from all over Israel and abroad gathered to prove themselves, each of us hoping to make it through one of the most demanding days of our lives.

I used to prepare a lot during my free time at Michve Alon. I'd go on short runs, squeeze in bodyweight workouts, and try to eat clean—even in a dining hall full of temptation. I took every moment seriously because I knew what was ahead. I wasn't just training for myself—I was preparing to prove I belonged among the best. And beyond the physical prep, I was studying Hebrew daily, reviewing flashcards, jotting new words into a notebook, and practicing conversations. I knew that the language barrier could hold me back just as much as any physical weakness.

When *Yom Sayarot* came, I gave it everything I had. We were tested on endurance, strength, and mental focus. Sprints, crawls, push-ups, leadership drills—nothing was easy, and every second counted. Soldiers around me started dropping, one by one, from exhaustion or injury. I kept pushing. I wanted to finish strong, no matter what.

By the end of the day, I was spent, but proud. I believed I had done well.

Then came the interview. The captain sat across from me and explained that while I had shown strong physical and mental qualities, my Hebrew wasn't yet fluent enough for their standards. He was kind but firm.

It hit hard. All that effort—and still, it wasn't enough.

Later, I found Ariel. He had been through the same process. He looked at me and said, "They said no. My Hebrew, too." We both just sat there in silence for a while.

But at that moment, something shifted. I realized that trying and falling short wasn't failure. It was courage. And sitting there with Ariel, knowing we both gave it everything, reminded me of why I started this journey in the first place. It wasn't just about making it into an elite unit. It was about growing into someone stronger than I had been the day before.

We didn't make it, but we weren't done.

A RENEWED COMMITMENT

Over the next few months, I committed myself to mastering Hebrew. I practiced daily, surrounded myself with fluent friends, listened to Hebrew music, and challenged myself to use the language constantly. Slowly, my confidence in Hebrew began to grow. By the time my next big test approached, I knew I was stronger—both in my language skills and in my physical endurance. This new challenge was the Gibush Achatiyot, also known as the selection day for Sayeret Nahal, the reconnaissance unit of the Nahal Brigade.

Sayeret Nahal is known not only for its exceptional combat skills but also for its deep roots in social commitment and community service—a legacy that dates back to the brigade's founding, when Nahal soldiers combined military duty with volunteering in pioneering communities. That unique balance between strength and purpose made the Nahal Brigade stand out to me, and I felt it was the right path to follow.

The requirements for Sayeret Nahal were just as intense as those for any elite unit selection. The tryout tested everything from long-distance runs and obstacle courses to mental toughness and teamwork drills that pushed us beyond our limits.

The morning of the Gibush Achatiyot, I could feel the tension in the air—a mix of excitement, fear, and determination. Every soldier there knew that only a few would make it through.

It was cold, and tension filled the air as all 280 of us stood waiting. The commanders circled us, laying out the rules and the risks. They warned us of the dangers—everything from heat stroke to hypothermia. They gave us one last chance to walk away, joking that there would be hot tea waiting for anyone who opted out. But I had no plans of backing down, and looking around, I saw the same determination on the faces of everyone else.

INTO THE COLD AND MUD

The exam began just as the sun went down, and, to add to the challenge, it began to rain. The ground quickly turned to thick slush, and the cold seeped through our soaked clothes as we crawled and sprinted through each new challenge. With each step, I could feel my body's energy draining, the mud making every movement feel like lifting weights. I slipped several times, my knees and hands sinking deep into the earth, but I pushed on, driven by sheer determination. At one point, the commanders sent us back to our tents, giving us a moment's break to change into dry uniforms. I felt a flicker of hope—maybe we'd get some rest. But within minutes, we were ordered back outside, back into the mud, the cold biting even harder this time. Each time we returned to our tents, I noticed our numbers were shrinking. Some of the soldiers couldn't take the conditions any longer and quietly gave up. Their spots remained empty, a reminder of how tough the demands truly were.

The following days were brutal. The temperature dropped even more, and each task grew harder. Our food was simple and scarce—mostly canned tuna, with only a few minutes to eat before the next test began. I remember a friend next to me, struggling to open his can, his hands shaking from the cold. In a moment of tired ingenuity, he mixed his tuna with a chocolate spread, calling it his "time-saving invention." We couldn't help but laugh at this bizarre combination; his humor kept us going when we couldn't bear any more. We learned quickly that time was precious; every second counted. Even small moments of levity like that one helped us push through the cold, the hunger, and the sheer physical demands of the tasks ahead.

A TEST OF WILLPOWER

The journey through Gibush Achatiyot was like no other challenge I'd faced before. The commanders seemed intent on testing not just our physical strength but the very core of who we were. The days blurred together with relentless marches through rough terrain, the weight of our gear pressing into our backs and shoulders like a constant reminder of what was at stake. Each step felt heavier than the last, every incline steeper than it looked.

The physical strain was immense, but the mental battle was where the real test lay. Pushing through pain required more than strength—it demanded focus, determination, and a constant reminder of why I had come to Israel in the first place. I kept replaying the promise I'd made to myself when I left Argentina: to contribute, to belong, and to prove that I was capable of enduring whatever challenges were placed before me.

What kept me going wasn't just my own resolve but the strength of those beside me. My fellow soldiers became my lifeline. We weren't competing; we were lifting each other, literally and figuratively. In moments of silence, when the weight of the mission bore down on us, a simple word of encouragement or a shared nod of understanding was enough to reignite that spark of determination.

When the final day of Gibush Achatiyot came, I was physically drained but mentally sharp. I'd carried my gear, followed every order, and pushed through the voice in my head that had whispered doubts along the way. As we lined up for one last debrief, I took a deep breath. I made it. Whether or not I had achieved what I'd set out to do, I had overcome the tests, both external and internal.

But what happened after the gibush ended was something I never expected. As we approached the base, I saw rows of soldiers lining the path ahead. They weren't just standing—they were clapping, cheering, and applauding every single one of us who had completed the gibush. It was as though the entire base had come out to honor what we had just been through.

Some soldiers reached out to give us high-fives, others nodded with quiet respect. For a moment, the exhaustion faded, replaced by an overwhelming sense of pride. Walking through that line felt like crossing a finish line I didn't even know I needed. The recognition reminded me that every drop of sweat, every moment of doubt, every painful step had been worth it.

I wasn't just walking through a line of soldiers; I was walking into a community that understood the value of endurance. It wasn't about who had performed the best; it was about the collective effort, the shared struggle, and the strength we had all shown.

MOVING FORWARD

Though the *gibush* didn't lead me exactly where I had hoped, it shaped me in ways I couldn't have anticipated. The lessons I'd learned—about grit, friendship, and inner strength—now became a part of my identity. My improved Hebrew allowed me to connect more deeply with those around me, and the friendships I'd formed gave me a sense of belonging that was stronger than ever.

As I left the *gibush* behind, I felt a deep sense of pride, knowing I had given everything I had. The day of the announcement was both nerve-wracking and electric—the air thick with tension and hope. Out of nearly 280 soldiers, only 108 were selected to move forward. As we gathered to hear the final names, I could feel the weight of anticipation pressing down on all of us. Then, when I finally heard my name called, it was as if a surge of relief and gratitude rushed through me. I threw my arms into the air, letting the pride of that moment sink in—knowing that every ounce of pain, exhaustion, and determination had been worth it.

The journey through Gibush Achatiyot was more than just a test of physical and mental strength—it was a defining chapter in my life. It showed me what I was capable of, taught me to lean on others, and reaffirmed the reason I had come to Israel. The path ahead was still uncertain, but I knew one thing for sure: whatever lay before me, I was ready to face it head-on.

CHAPTER 6
FINDING STRENGTH IN SUPPORT

From the moment I joined this unit, the intensity of the commitment was clear. Training was relentless, especially at the start, when every drill, every instruction, and every order felt new and challenging. The language barrier made things even harder; instructions came fast and in Hebrew, often leaving me struggling to keep up. But I quickly realized I wasn't alone. Some of the soldiers in my unit noticed my difficulties and helped translate or explain the parts I missed. That camaraderie became essential, reminding me that in this environment, we had to rely on each other to get through.

One of the toughest parts was learning how to manage time with military precision. Every task had a strict timer, and if we missed it by even a second, we had to start over. There was no room for error. Each night, we'd go through the "two-bet" routine: we'd lay out our uniforms and boots beside our beds so we'd be ready to leap up, get dressed, and line up outside in full formation within two minutes. In those early days, we failed again and again, missing the mark by just a few seconds. But after more than twenty attempts, we finally got it right, lining up perfectly on time. It was a small victory, but one that made us feel united, proving that we were becoming a team.

THE MORNING ROUTINE

Our mornings began at full speed. The instant we woke up, we had only six minutes to brush our teeth and complete our morning hygiene routine. Half-asleep, I'd rush through it, barely having time to think before we were outside, running at top speed. When we returned, the pace didn't let up; more orders came at us, demanding every bit of energy we had.

One of the toughest routines was the "seven-up" drill. From the moment the commander started the clock, chaos erupted. We had exactly seven minutes to sprint to our barracks, strip off our uniforms, and race to the showers—only eight showers for nearly forty soldiers. I remember one guy standing right in the middle, pouring shampoo over everyone who ran past, shouting reminders that the commanders would literally smell our hair afterward to make sure we'd showered properly. Some tried to skip it, hoping to get away with a quick rinse, but there was no hiding from inspection.

Once done, we'd sprint back from the showers, dripping wet, struggling to pull on our uniforms over damp skin. Every second mattered. If even one soldier wasn't in perfect formation when time ran out, the whole drill restarted. Again and again, we'd repeat it until everyone made it on time. Exhausting as it was, it drilled into us one unshakable lesson: we succeed—or fail—together. When we finally stood ready, side by side, it felt less like survival and more like unity.

Gradually, I found my footing. I pushed myself hard in every physical test, especially during the runs. Each three-kilometer run was a test of willpower, and I wanted to prove that I was committed. Determined to finish first, I'd sprint with everything I had, crossing the finish line gasping for air, sometimes on the verge of collapse. But each time I did, I felt a sense of pride, knowing that I was giving my best. My teammates noticed, too, and the respect I earned from them was worth every step.

THE CHALLENGES OF BEING A LONE SOLDIER

As a lone soldier, everything was different for me. Not everyone understood what it meant to serve without family nearby. While some of my fellow soldiers were curious and kind, asking about my background and why I'd come all this way, others were more skeptical. A few joked, "Why not just stay back home on a couch, sipping a coffee?" Explaining my reasons wasn't always easy. For some, it was hard to grasp that my commitment came from something deeply personal—a connection to my heritage and a profound sense of duty. Over time, though, I believe they began to see my resolve and started to respect my decision.

One memory that has stayed with me was a particularly grueling training session at an undisclosed location. The area was filled with empty structures, and we were tasked with training as a unit to navigate and clear them in silence, as though there was an enemy threat inside. The whole day and night—nearly 36 hours without sleep—were spent practicing strategies, improving teamwork, and undergoing physically demanding exercises.

The goal of the training was clear: to break us down mentally and physically so that we could be rebuilt into stronger, more capable combat soldiers. It was relentless, and by the morning, we were drained. But the most challenging task was still ahead of us.

Our final mission was a stretcher run—a competition against other units. We had to carry the stretcher with the heaviest soldier in our unit across several kilometers of difficult terrain. The weight was immense, but we kept a strong pace, staying focused and working together.

As we neared the finish line, the unthinkable happened. The stretcher slipped from our hands and fell, the weight crashing down onto the ground. I froze for a split second, the cheers from the crowd ahead muffled by the pounding in my ears. Then, without hesitation, I grabbed one of the handles, shouted for my team to get up, and motivated everyone to push forward. We lifted the stretcher together and crossed the finish line, greeted by the sound of applause and cheering.

To my surprise, the crowd wasn't just made up of soldiers—it was filled with the parents of my fellow unit members. The commanders had invited them to witness this moment, knowing how intense the training had been. The parents stood there, clapping and smiling, their faces filled with pride as they saw their sons emerging as strong combat soldiers.

I closed my eyes for a brief moment, imagining my own family in that crowd, clapping and hugging me. I could see their smiles, feel their arms around me. But when I opened my eyes, the reality hit me—my family wasn't there. Tears welled up in my eyes, and I couldn't hold them back.

One of the other lone soldiers in my unit, a kindhearted guy from Colombia, noticed what I was going through. Without saying a word, he came over, tears in his eyes, and hugged me. Soon, other soldiers joined, and some even invited me to meet their families and share a meal with them.

The warmth and consideration of my unit left me speechless. A few families even approached me directly, asking if I had a place to spend Shabbat that weekend. "Come join us," they said. "We'd love to have you."

In that moment, I felt something I hadn't expected—a sense of belonging that transcended bloodlines. The generosity and unity of those around me reminded me that even though I was far from home, I wasn't alone. It was one of the best feelings in the world.

Unlike other lone soldiers, I didn't have an adoptive family assigned to me when I arrived in Israel. My story unfolded differently. Surprisingly, it was my Hebrew teacher who first welcomed me into her family. She introduced me to her loved ones, and over time, they became my adoptive family. I hadn't realized how much I needed this kind of support until it was there. They gave me strength on the toughest days, and their presence became a constant reminder of why I had chosen this path.

THE YAVIN FAMILY: A HOME AWAY FROM HOME

I first met the Yavin family through my Hebrew tutor, Yam. From the moment we started our lessons, Yam was more than just a teacher—she was incredibly patient and genuinely invested in helping me succeed. I was just beginning to learn the language, stumbling over the alphabet and struggling to form basic sentences, but she always encouraged me to keep going. She paid close attention to my progress and never gave up on me, even when I was frustrated with myself.

As our lessons continued, Yam began sharing stories about me with her family. Maybe it was the effort I put into learning Hebrew, or the fact that I was a lone soldier who had come from abroad to serve in the army. Whatever it was, something about my story stuck with her—and eventually, she invited me to join her family for Shabbat dinner.

When I arrived at their home for the first time, I was met at the door by Yam's mother and siblings. Without hesitation, they hugged me like I was already part of the family. There was no awkwardness, no distance—just warmth. The fact that they knew I was serving in the army, protecting people like them, meant the world to them. But to me, it meant even more that they welcomed me so openly without knowing much about me at all.

Reef, one of Yam's brothers who was just about to turn 18 and begin his own army service, became someone I quietly tried to set an example for. I knew that my presence in their home wasn't just about comfort—it carried meaning. I wanted Reef to see that serving could be done with strength and heart. We spoke a few times before his draft, and I tried to pass along the kind of guidance I would've wanted at that age—not just about physical training, but about mindset, brotherhood, and resilience. I wanted to be someone his family could look at and say, "That's the kind of soldier we hope our son becomes."

From that night on, the Yavins became more than just hosts; they became my second family.

Each time I arrived at their door after a long week of training, covered in dust and weighed down by gear, I knew I'd be met with warmth, hugs, and a feeling of belonging. They never treated me like a guest. I was just another part of their household. And that meant everything.

They helped me with everything—from meals to laundry—and gave me a space to rest and reset. For those short weekends off base, I wasn't a soldier. I was a brother, a friend, a son. The kids looked up to me and asked questions about what it was like in the army, and I shared my experiences with honesty and care. I knew how important these conversations could be, especially for young Israelis about to enter service themselves.

FINDING COMFORT IN SIMPLE ROUTINES

In their home, the routines we shared brought me comfort. I'd help clean the floors, wash dishes, or lend a hand wherever I could. These small tasks reminded me of my family back in New

Jersey and helped me feel closer to home. I could almost hear my mom in the background, telling one of my siblings to stop watching TV and help set the table. Whenever I mentioned helping out around the house to my family on a call, my siblings would joke, "As long as you're not breaking the broom again," or "Please tell me you're not entrusted with the good plates!" The only difference this time was that I wasn't breaking anything. No cracked dishes, no snapped mop handles, just me, doing my part. It was my quiet way of giving back to the Yavins for all they were giving me—a place to recharge, to feel grounded, and to be cared for in a country that was still new, but beginning to feel more and more like home.

Every lone soldier deserves the kind of warmth and support that the Yavins gave me. Their home became my safe haven, a place where I could find relief from the intensity of military life. It made all the difference, providing a foundation of support that helped me face the many challenges of training.

THE STRENGTH OF SUPPORT

The bond with the Yavin family, combined with the friendships I was building on base, helped me endure the most difficult days. Training was intense, demanding everything I had, but knowing I had people by my side, both on and off base, kept me going. My fellow soldiers became my second family in their own way, each of us supporting one another as we pushed through the seemingly impossible routines. As tough as things got, the support I received reminded me of why I had chosen this path. I wanted to serve, to find a deeper connection to my heritage, and to test my limits. With the Yavins and my fellow soldiers backing me up, I felt stronger than I ever thought possible. No matter how grueling the training was, the sense of purpose and the strength I found in my support network made me realize I was exactly where I was meant to be.

CHAPTER 7
A NEW CHAPTER IN COMBAT

Training was intense, but nothing felt quite as rewarding as completing it. After months of hard work and countless challenges, I was finally at the end of my training and on the edge of becoming a fully qualified combat soldier. The final test was one we'd all been waiting for: a fifty-kilometer march, each of us carrying heavy bags that seemed to weigh down not just our shoulders but our very spirits. Every step was a battle against fatigue, but we pushed through, determined. This was the last push, the final challenge that would earn us the right to wear the green beret—a symbol that meant everything. It marked the transition from being trainees to soldiers, from those learning to those ready to defend.

Everything moved quickly after that. I was stationed in Hebron, a city in the West Bank with a history as deep as its streets were dangerous. Hebron was home to both Palestinians and a small Jewish community. The city was tense, filled with a mix of old stone buildings, bustling markets, and alleys that twisted and turned unpredictably. Our job as soldiers was clear: maintain peace, prevent violence, and protect the people living there. But there was always an edge to the calm; you could feel it, an invisible line that could be crossed at any moment, sparking chaos. In those early weeks, we were sent out on missions almost as soon as we arrived. Every day brought new challenges. We would move through narrow streets, sometimes searching houses for weapons, sometimes gathering intelligence. It wasn't easy, and the risks were real, but the work was necessary. The days began to blur, one mission after another, the weight of my gear becoming a constant companion.

A HOLIDAY LIKE NO OTHER

October 6, 2023, was the holiday of Simchat Torah, a day meant for celebration. In Israel, this holiday is a time of singing, dancing, and community. It marks the completion of reading the Torah and the start of reading it again, symbolizing a joyful cycle. My unit was on its way back from a successful week of missions, walking down a hill as the sky shifted from bright blue to warm shades of orange and pink. The feeling among us was light, even happy. We were looking forward to joining the families in a nearby village and taking part in the festivities. When we arrived, the scene was heartwarming. At least a hundred children, with faces lit up with excitement, ran toward us. They each held small Torah scrolls and danced, their energy contagious. The air was filled with laughter and song, and for a moment, the harsh realities of our duties melted away. The warmth of the families reminded us why we were there—to protect moments like these.

Saying goodbye took a while, with so many kids wanting to talk and share their happiness. But eventually, we made our way back to base. The walk was quieter, filled with the kind of reflective silence that comes after a special moment. Some of the soldiers started conversations about life outside the military, while others, like me, walked in silence, savoring the peace. I fell into bed that night, grateful for the simple joys, convinced I would finally get a decent sleep.

THE ALARM OF REALITY

At around 07:00 the next morning, shouts and hurried footsteps woke me. The base was in chaos; soldiers were rushing around, shouting news that was hard to comprehend. We had been attacked. Terrorists had broken through into Israel, and rockets were falling on our towns. The information was jumbled, and no one seemed to have a clear idea of the full scale of the situation. My phone buzzed with message after message from friends, family, and our volunteer soldiers' WhatsApp group. The texts were a flurry of concern and confusion: *Are you safe? Are you okay?*

On the morning of October 7, 2023, Israel faced one of the deadliest and most coordinated attacks in its modern history. At dawn, around 06:30, Hamas launched a surprise assault from Gaza. Over 2,000 terrorists breached the border at multiple points, infiltrating Israeli communities, military bases, and public areas. Simultaneously, thousands of rockets were fired toward civilian cities, overwhelming the Iron Dome system.

They attacked by land, air, and sea—storming towns, burning homes, taking hostages, and killing families in their beds. The brutality was unimaginable. It was unlike anything Israel had seen in decades.

I glanced around and saw the same bewildered look on everyone's face. We were all trying to process what was happening, but the pieces didn't fit together. That's when our high-ranking commander entered the room, his voice sharp and commanding. "Everyone, formation, now!" he shouted. The room fell silent as we lined up. He stood before us, a stern look on his face. "Listen up. The situation is developing, and intelligence is still coming in," he began. He listed the areas where terrorists had infiltrated and warned us that there were strong signs that local terror cells in Hebron could mobilize. Our base was potentially at risk. "Get your vests, ammunition, and gear," he ordered. "We're heading out to Kiryat Arba to defend the village until further notice." Kiryat Arba was a small settlement on the edge of Hebron. It was known for its resilient community, but was also a frequent target of unrest due to its location. Protecting it meant putting ourselves directly in the line of potential conflict.

A NIGHT OF VIGILANCE

The hours that followed were a blur of movement and tension. We arrived in Kiryat Arba and spread out, securing the perimeter and standing guard. The day slipped into night, and fatigue clawed at me, but there was no time for rest. We had to stay alert. Every shadow, every noise, felt like a potential threat. My thoughts kept returning to the children we had danced with just the day before, wondering if they were safe.

As the sky began to lighten with the first hints of morning, my commander approached me with hurried steps. His face was serious, eyes locked onto mine.

"Daniel, come with me," he said, pulling me aside. I followed him, a sense of dread building in my chest.

"Listen, Daniel," he continued, his tone hard but steady. "Our unit's only machine gunner is an only son. His mother has requested that he be removed from this duty."

I had heard of this before—how the IDF grants the request of a parent to pull their only child from combat roles. It's a policy rooted in deep national pain and tradition. If a parent makes that call, it is honored—no questions asked.

I barely had time to process before my commander handed me the weapon.

My breath caught as I realized what he was saying. The machine gunner's role was critical. Armed with the FN MAG, a 7.62 mm machine gun weighing 11 kilograms (24 pounds) unloaded—and nearly twice that when fully equipped with ammunition—the gun was a powerhouse on the battlefield. Known for its adaptability, the FN MAG could lay down continuous suppressive fire or deliver precision shots when mounted on a bipod. During the Yom Kippur War, it had even been used as a sniper rifle in some battles before transitioning to its full role as a machine gun, proving its reliability under pressure. It could provide cover for an entire team or hold off multiple threats when it mattered most. And now, it was mine to carry.

He placed it in my arms. The cold weight of it sank into my chest.

"Good luck," he said, giving me a firm pat on the back. "You're the new machine gunner. You'll be on a bus to the training base in thirty minutes. You have one day to train."

I nodded, still silent. The physical burden of the weapon was heavy, but it was the responsibility that truly hit me.

I had eight siblings. I wasn't an only child. I knew my parents worried about me, but I also knew they understood why I was here. I had called my dad earlier to tell him about my new position. He told me I'd be fine. That it would build me into a stronger man. But inside, I was afraid. What if I wasn't ready? What if I made a mistake?

Thirty minutes later, I was sitting on the bus, the FN MAG across my lap, staring out at the passing hills. Everything felt distant—like the world was moving, but I wasn't in it.

THE LOSS OF A FRIEND

As the bus rumbled down the road, the reality of my new role sank in. My phone buzzed with new messages from the volunteer soldiers' group, each one repeating the same ominous words: *"Nathanel is not with us anymore."* At first, it didn't register. The words blurred together until a video appeared on my screen. The footage showed the aftermath of an attack on Nahal Oz, an IDF base near the Gaza border. It was a key post, positioned close to the heart of conflict zones, always at risk due to its proximity to Gaza and the ongoing threat from Hamas. My stomach twisted as I realized that Nathanel, a friend I had shared so many moments with, had been stationed there. The video confirmed the worst. He was gone, taken by the violence that had erupted while we celebrated Simchat Torah. I felt the world shift, the bus seat under me hard and unyielding as the news settled in. The gun at my feet seemed heavier than before, a reminder that nothing about this was a dream. It was reality, harsh and unforgiving. The bus continued down the road, carrying me to my new duty and deeper into a chapter of life that would test me in ways I could never have imagined.

CHAPTER 8
REMEMBERING NATHANEL YOUNG Z"L

first met Nathanel Young at Michve Alon, where we studied Hebrew together. From the start, Nat stood out. He had this calm confidence, an easy smile, and a way of making you feel like things were going to be okay, even when they weren't. That mattered a lot back then, when everything around us felt new and uncertain. We became friends quickly. What bonded us wasn't just the shared experience of being lone soldiers—it was the late-night talks, the jokes during long marches, the honest moments.

I'll never forget the last time I saw him. It was by chance—on a train ride home. I was tired, drained from a weekend of training, and there he was. We locked eyes, smiled, and before long, we were sitting side by side, trading stories from our respective units. He was proud of the work he was doing. I could hear it in his voice—he believed in what he was doing, and it made me think about why I was here, too. Before I got off the train, we hugged. He said, "We need to catch up more," and I agreed. I really thought we would.

But we never got that chance.

On October 7, I got the news that Nathanel had been killed in the attack on his base near Gaza. At first, I couldn't believe it. I kept thinking about that last conversation—how alive he was, how full of energy and purpose. It didn't feel real.

Then it did. And it hit hard.

That day, my mind was spiraling with grief, confusion, and a strange kind of clarity. I remembered a moment weeks earlier when one of the mothers in our unit had pulled her only son from the role of machine gunner, worried for his safety. At the time, I didn't fully understand it. Part of me had seen it as fear. But now, standing in the shadow of Nathanel's death, I began to see something else in her decision—love, maybe even wisdom.

Would any mother choose differently, knowing the cost?

It didn't make me regret my own path, but it forced me to think about the unbearable weight parents carry when they send their children into war. That mother may have been right. Or maybe there is no right or wrong in these moments—just impossible choices that leave you haunted either way.

There's something about losing someone so close that cracks something open in you. I didn't just grieve Nat—I carried a weight I couldn't explain. I couldn't sleep. I replayed everything. I kept asking myself why. Why would someone so kind, so full of life, be taken like that? Why someone who wanted nothing more than to protect others would be the one lost.

He didn't deserve this. None of them did.

And yet, the war doesn't ask, "What's fair?" It just takes.

What changed in me after Nat's death was deeper than grief—it was responsibility. I felt like I had to live for him now. To serve harder. To protect his people—his friends, his family—as if they were my own. I couldn't explain it then, but it was like I had been handed something the day he died. A piece of his mission. His courage. His light.

I carry it with me.

Nathanel was from Southgate, London. His roots were deep in the Jewish community there. He made *aliyah* to follow a calling, a need to give back to the people he loved and the country he believed in. He worked at the Hilton, DJed in Tel Aviv, and trained for combat. He was all in. And I saw that fire in him every time we spoke. He believed in the cause, and he backed it up with action.

He lived by a quote, which he had hanging on his wall:

> "Some people want it to happen, some wish it could happen, others make it happen."

Nat was the one who made it happen.

Now it's on me, and on all of us, to carry that message forward.

Since he passed, I've felt moments where I've wanted to give up or slow down. But I remember him. And I remind myself: I'm still here. And I have a duty—not just as a soldier, but as a friend. To keep showing up. To serve with honor. To live a life that would make him proud.

I miss him more than words can express. But through every mission, every challenge, and every moment of doubt, I carry him with me. Nathanel's name may be etched into stone now, but his legacy is alive in the way we live, the way we protect, and the way we love each other fiercely and without apology.

He was a hero. He is a hero.

And I'll spend the rest of my life trying to live like one, for him.

I miss you every day, Nathanel Young. Thank you for being the friend you were to me and for the example you set. Your memory lives on in all of us.

CHAPTER 9
A HEAVY WEIGHT

The bus ride to the training base was unlike any other. With every mile, I felt the pressure building—this was no ordinary journey. My phone buzzed constantly, delivering a flood of notifications that I couldn't keep up with. Updates on the situation at the Gaza border, messages from friends checking in, and frantic texts from my family back home trying to understand what was happening. It was overwhelming. I had only been on this new path for a short time, yet I was already faced with a reality I hadn't fully prepared for.

Sitting there with the machine gun at my feet, the weight of it all pressed down on me. I barely knew how to use this weapon, and here I was heading toward a place where that knowledge would be crucial. A war was unfolding right in front of us, with battles raging at the Gaza border. I had already lost friends, and the worry that more would be taken weighed on me heavily. My family didn't grasp the full extent of what was happening, and even if I wanted to explain, I wouldn't have known how. The messages, each more urgent than the last, swirled together in my mind, forming a chaotic blend of worry, fear, and duty. For a moment, it all felt like too much. I took a deep breath, forcing myself to pause, to quiet the storm in my mind. I remembered my responsibility—to be strong, to push my emotions aside for the time being. This was something we were trained to do in combat; we learned to compartmentalize, to set feelings aside in order to stay focused. I'd have to save my emotions for later. Right now, there was no space for hesitation. I needed to be ready, both mentally and physically, and somehow, I found a sense of calm in that decision. At that moment, I became numb, not because I didn't feel, but because I had to shut it all out to survive.

ARRIVING AT THE BASE

When the bus pulled into the base, I was greeted quickly with a salute and escorted to a room. Inside, an officer handed me a five-page packet that outlined every single part of the machine gun I'd be responsible for. It was detailed, intimidating, and I felt the weight of what I was about to take on. They wasted no time getting me started—I was to learn the weapon inside-out, from every tiny part to how to assemble and disassemble it. The first task was straightforward on paper but challenging in practice: take the gun apart, then put it back together as fast as possible. I struggled at first, my fingers clumsy over the unfamiliar parts, the clock ticking as I worked. My first attempt was slow, and I could feel my frustration building with each mistake. But with every repetition, my movements grew more fluid. I learned to focus on each part, to work with precision and speed. After a few tries, I felt a small flicker of confidence as I clicked the pieces back into place with ease. The trainers were patient but firm, reminding me of the details I missed and encouraging me to work faster. I stayed focused, determined to get it right. After a few hours of intense practice, one of the trainers gave me a nod of approval, signaling that it was time to head to the shooting range.

THE FIRST SHOT

By the time we reached the range, the afternoon sun was starting to dip, casting a warm light over everything. My trainer showed me to my spot and walked me through the basics of handling a machine gun: breathing, aiming, and positioning. He explained that accuracy wasn't just about sight but about staying calm and steady. He pointed to a spot 300 meters away and told me to build a small tower of rocks. That would be my target. I knelt down, gathering stones and stacking them carefully, then walked back to my position. Lying flat on the ground, I shouldered the machine gun, feeling the weight of it settle against me. I adjusted my aim, focusing on the tower in the distance. The trainer gave me the green light to fire, and I took one deep breath, letting my body relax. With a firm grip, I squeezed the trigger, and a burst of shots rang out, powerful enough to push my shoulder back forcefully. The rocks exploded in a cloud of dust, crumbling as the rounds tore through them, leaving nothing intact. I felt a strange satisfaction seeing the tower collapse, a sense of focus and anger mixed together. For a moment, everything else faded, and I felt only the intense clarity of those shots. We continued practicing through the afternoon and into the evening, each burst sharpening my aim and dulling the chaos in my mind. The steady rhythm of firing, breathing, and reloading was almost meditative, each round grounding me and channeling my emotions into something I could control. The frustration, the fear, and the sorrow—they blended into a solid determination to learn this weapon and use it to the best of my ability.

A NEW RESOLVE

As night fell, we returned to the barracks, and I finally lay down on my bunk, tired from the day's training. I was no longer the same person who had boarded that bus, weighed down by fear and uncertainty. I had a role to play now, and a weapon I was responsible for. I couldn't control the chaos outside, but I could control my focus, my training, and my determination. Tomorrow would bring more challenges, but for tonight, I knew I was ready.

A HEAVY WEIGHT

And then, just before I drifted off, my phone rang.

It had been a few days since I'd heard from Ariel—one of my closest friends in the army, someone I had instantly connected with during our early days of training. When I picked up the phone, his voice came through sharp and fast. He didn't even say hello. He just launched into it.

"Daniel ... we went straight to Kfar Aza," he said. His voice was tight, like he hadn't slept. Kfar Aza is a small kibbutz near the Gaza border, one of the hardest-hit communities during the October 7 attack.

He explained that when his unit arrived, they encountered several terrorists hiding among the homes. In one house, they were tasked with clearing the rooms—checking if anyone was still inside. That's when it happened.

As they entered a small bedroom, a terrorist opened fire.

Ariel's voice dropped.

"He shot Yotam ... right in front of me."

Yotam Hillel Z"L, a soldier who had trained with both of us, someone we had shared meals with, laughed with, trained beside, had gone in an instant.

I couldn't speak. I just sat there listening to Ariel breathe on the other end of the line. I could feel the shock in his voice—the kind of trauma that doesn't even have the words yet. And all I could think was: how does anyone move forward after witnessing something like that?

We both knew Yotam. He was quiet and kind, strong yet humble. A good soul was gone.

We didn't say much after that. There was nothing left to say. But before we hung up, we made a promise: that we would take care of ourselves—not just to survive, but so that someday we could be together again. We would then lift weights like we used to, eat pizza, and talk about life like we always did. That promise became something I held onto in the days that followed.

CHAPTER 10
THE CALM BEFORE THE STORM

T he morning air was heavy with tension as I woke up to new orders. We were told to pack our gear and prepare to head north, to an open field near Nahariya. Nahariya sits along Israel's northern coastline, just a few miles from the Lebanese border. It's a small town, beautiful yet strategic, close enough to Lebanon to serve as a key point if things escalated with Hezbollah. The orders were clear: we were to be ready for anything, prepared to move at a moment's notice. Once we boarded the bus, each of us carrying our heavy equipment, the officers handed out food and drinks for the trip. The mood was quiet, each of us lost in our thoughts. Outside the window, the landscape blurred by, but my mind was focused on what lay ahead. With everything happening around us—the war, the alerts, and now this new mission—the reality was setting in. It wasn't just training anymore; we were part of something big, something unpredictable.

A WARM WELCOME

When we finally arrived in the open field near Nahariya, we were met with a sight that filled me with unexpected warmth. People from nearby communities had come out to greet us, carrying homemade food, water, and whatever they could spare. They welcomed us with hugs, words of encouragement, and genuine kindness. For me, a lone soldier, those hugs meant more than they could know. In that moment, I felt deeply connected to the people around me, reminded of why we were here. These weren't just strangers—they were the people we were protecting. After a while, the locals said their goodbyes, leaving us to settle into our makeshift camp. I found a spot under a tree and unrolled my sleeping bag, trying to make myself comfortable on the hard ground. As I lay there, staring up at the branches above, I felt a strange mix of calm and anticipation. This wasn't home, but for now, it was the closest thing we had.

SIRENS IN THE NIGHT

Just as I started to settle in, a sharp siren shattered the quiet. The announcement came swiftly: there had been a drone infiltration. Without hesitation, we scrambled to take cover, moving quickly across the field. It became clear that this was only the beginning. Not long after, the next siren sounded, and this time, we looked up to see rockets streaking across the sky. Bright lines of light sliced through the dark, intercepted by the Iron Dome, exploding in flashes overhead. The sight was a reminder of the dangers that surrounded us. We barely slept that night. We caught maybe two hours of light sleep, and even that was only a restless doze, every sound keeping us on edge. Every time I closed my eyes, I felt the tension of being ready to move in an instant, the pressure of being constantly aware.

CHANGING COURSE

When morning came, new orders awaited us. Our mission had changed: we were heading to Nitzanim, a location just a few kilometers from the Gaza border. Nitzanim was even closer to the conflict, and the change in location signaled that things were heating up. We were told to prepare for the possibility of entering Gaza. The loud, steady chop of helicopter blades filled the air as the choppers arrived to transport us. The wind whipped through the field as the helicopters descended, creating a powerful gust that nearly knocked me off balance. We were commanded to move quickly, sprinting toward the helicopters. As I climbed aboard, adrenaline surged through me, my heart racing with a mix of excitement and fear. The roar of the engine was deafening, drowning out every other sound. I couldn't hear a thing, only the pulse of the rotors as we lifted off into the sky. When we landed in Nitzanim, we assembled in formation, awaiting further instructions. They led us to a secluded area where we would remain for the foreseeable future. Here, we were officially in a holding pattern, waiting for the next steps. It was clear: this was where we would be until the command came to move into Gaza.

THE CALM BEFORE THE STORM

The two weeks that followed were filled with intense, strategic training led by high-ranking commando units. These weren't just ordinary drills; they were designed to prepare us for the specifics of urban combat. Our commanders drilled us on everything from tactical maneuvers to communication strategies, teaching us how to handle the unexpected. We were also briefed on what to do if we encountered a terrorist alive, laying out every step of that difficult scenario. They stressed the importance of staying calm, reminding us that no matter what we saw, we needed to keep a level head. As part of our preparation, we had frequent sessions with psychologists. They explained the mental challenges we might face, preparing us to recognize signs of trauma or PTSD, whether in ourselves or in each other. One of the psychologists made a statement that stayed with me: *"No amount of training can prepare a soldier for war until he actually goes through it."* Those words sank in deeply. I looked around the room, scanning the faces of my fellow soldiers, my brothers. We were all just young men, most of us barely out of high school, tasked with defending our country and our families. In that moment, the weight of our responsibility felt more real than ever. During rare breaks, our group would gather in a circle, one of the guys bringing out his guitar. We'd sing together, letting the music drown out the intensity around us, if only for a few minutes. But even those moments of relief couldn't keep the heavy conversations away. One night, reality hit hard as we talked openly about the possibility that not everyone would come back. It was a truth we all understood but hadn't spoken out loud. Yet, as the days passed, it became impossible to ignore.

GIFTS OF UNITY AND REMEMBRANCE

During those two weeks, each of us was given an Israeli flag. The gesture was simple yet powerful, a reminder of the unity and strength that held us all together. As I held the flag, an idea struck me. I took a pen and began writing down the names of my family members and closest friends on the fabric, one by one, until each name was there. I left a large space in one corner and carefully wrote down the names of my close friends who had already fallen during the early days of the war. This flag became a deeply personal keepsake, a silent reminder of everyone I was fighting for and everyone I wanted to protect. I also found a pocket-sized journal and pen, which fit perfectly into the inner top pocket of my bulletproof vest. With the flag carrying the names of those who mattered most and the journal ready to capture any thoughts or moments I couldn't say aloud, I felt a strange sense of confidence. No matter what happened, I knew this was an experience I would carry with me forever.

THE FINAL FAREWELL

As our departure drew closer, our commanders took away our phones at times, cutting us off from the outside world to ensure we stayed focused. But eventually, they gave us one final opportunity to contact our families. We were instructed to keep the conversations brief and to avoid giving away any specific details. When I heard my parents' voices on the other end, I felt a wave of emotion I struggled to keep down. I imagined them all gathered around the phone, their worry evident in every word they spoke. My voice was steady, but I could hear the understanding in theirs—they knew what was coming. My younger siblings each took a turn, telling me to stay safe, their voices full of innocence and hope. With a heavy heart, I said my goodbyes, keeping it brief, as the officers had instructed. After the call, we were told to write our full names and emergency contact information on the backs of our phones. We placed them into a large metal box, locked away as if symbolizing the end of one chapter and the start of another.

THE ROAD TO THE BORDER

That afternoon, I walked down to where the buses were lined up, my machine gun slung over my shoulder. As I made my way, fellow soldiers patted my back, nodding in silent support, cheering me on with small gestures that spoke volumes. Their encouragement lifted my spirits, filling me with a strange mix of pride and resolve. For that moment, I felt like I was exactly where I needed to be, part of something bigger than myself. We boarded the bus, each of our names checked off the list as we took our seats. The bus was packed, filled with the murmurs of conversation and quiet anticipation. Soon, someone started a song, and we all joined in, our voices rising together in unison. Each verse felt like a declaration, an unspoken promise of strength and solidarity. As the bus rolled toward the border, I stared out the window, absorbing every detail of the landscape, every passing tree, every stretch of road. It was hard to believe what was coming. This was real—our training, our unity, everything we had prepared for was about to be tested. As we drew closer to our destination, the weight of our mission settled over me fully. The uncertainty loomed, but in that moment, surrounded by my brothers, I knew I wasn't alone. Whatever lay ahead, we would face it together, one step at a time.

PART ONE
THE JOURNAL

October 29, 2023
Near the Gaza Border

When I slipped that small journal into the top pocket of my bulletproof vest, I wasn't just packing gear—I was making a promise to myself. I'd write every day, no matter what. Even if I was exhausted, terrified, or too numb to feel anything at all, I'd still find a way to put something down. I needed to.

There were two reasons.

The first was simple—if I didn't make it out, this journal would. Maybe someone would find it and finally understand what we lived through. Not just the chaos of war, but the fear, the brotherhood, and the quiet moments that revealed our humanity.

The second reason was for me. If I did make it home, I didn't want those memories to blur into distant stories I could barely recall. I wanted to remember the faces, the sounds, the emotions—everything as it truly was. Writing became a way to hold on to what was real, to keep it from slipping away. Maybe one day, I thought, I'd turn it into something bigger—a way to honor the people I served with, and the ones who never made it back.

That first day, October 29th, we were just two kilometers from the border. I'd never felt so alert. Everything was loud—helicopters roaring overhead, rockets being intercepted mid-air by the Iron Dome, the constant buzz of orders coming in over radios. But inside, I was quiet. Not calm, just quiet. Like I was bracing for something I couldn't name.

We were going to be the first ones to go in on foot. That thought settled in my stomach like lead. I looked around at the guys next to me—everyone wore the same expression: focused, afraid, pretending not to be. I wasn't sure what I was feeling. It wasn't panic, but it wasn't courage either. It was something in between —a readiness that came when there was no other choice.

I pulled out the journal and opened it to the first page. My hands were trembling—not from fear, but from the weight of knowing I had to put this into words. What do you even write when you're about to step into war?

> *"We are less than two kilometers from the border. Helicopters above. Rockets being intercepted. All I feel is anxiety and appreciation for this beautiful life I have."*

That was it—honest and simple. But in those two lines, I had captured everything I couldn't say out loud. I was afraid—afraid of dying, of not being strong enough. I was confused about what the next few hours would bring. And yet, beneath it all, I felt something else too: gratitude. Gratitude for my life, and for the fact that I could care so deeply that losing it scared me.

That journal became more than a habit. It was my lifeline. My release. It became the one place I could tell the truth without worrying what anyone else thought. The one place where I didn't need to be the tough guy with the machine gun—I could just be Daniel. A kid from New Jersey, scared but trying to be brave. Trying to make sense of something way bigger than me.

People talk about war stripping everything away. They're right. You lose track of time, of sleep, of comfort. But for me, I didn't want to lose track of *myself*. That's what the journal was for. To hold on to who I was. To remember why I came here. To remind myself, one page at a time, that even in the middle of chaos, we're still human.

I zipped it back into my vest, took a breath, and got back in line. The border was near. I didn't know what was coming. But I knew I'd be writing about it if I was lucky enough to see tomorrow.

THE ENTRANCE

30/10/23
3:30 AM

"We just crossed into Gaza. Explosions and tank fire all around—the ground shaking, the air thick with smoke. Being this close to the sea feels strange, like standing between two worlds, neither of them safe. Then it happened—a flash of light from a small building and gunfire. 'Face that way and guard!' my commander shouted. I dropped fast, swung my gun around, and aimed. My heart was pounding so hard I could hear it over the shots. The tanks fired back. Dust everywhere. Then silence. We checked each other—no one was hit. We kept walking through the rubble, backs aching, heads down. Just the sound of our boots and the war still echoing in the distance."

The border loomed ahead of us in the early morning darkness, an invisible line dividing what we knew from the unknown. It was October 30, 2023, and everything we had trained for led to this moment. The air felt suffocating, thick with tension, as if it carried the weight of the conflict waiting on the other side. We had been briefed, prepared, and conditioned for weeks, but no amount of preparation could capture what it felt like to take those first steps.

At 3:30 AM, we entered Gaza.

The darkness was overwhelming, broken only by bursts of light from tank fire and explosions. Each flash illuminated the barren landscape, casting fleeting shadows that made it impossible to tell what was real and what was imagined. The noise was deafening—shells roaring, distant gunfire cracking, and the ground beneath us trembling with every impact. It felt as though the earth itself was alive, warning us with its unrelenting vibrations.

Our high-ranking commander had gathered us before we crossed the border. In a firm, steady voice, he reminded us why we were here.

"Our mission," he said, "is to bring the hostages back to their families and to protect one another. We will not enter Gaza the way Hamas entered Israel. We are soldiers of the IDF. We have honor, and we have purpose. You are not just fighting for yourselves—you are fighting for the people who are counting on you to make it home."

His words struck a deep chord within me. This wasn't about vengeance. It wasn't about unleashing chaos. It was about precision, control, and humanity—values that separated us from the brutality we had seen unleashed on our own people.

Before moving forward, we said the *Shema Yisrael* together, a prayer that has been a source of strength for Jews throughout history, especially in moments of danger. It's a declaration of faith, a plea for protection, and a reminder of unity. In that moment, it bound us together, giving us the strength to face whatever lay ahead.

CROSSING THE LINE

The massive border fence stretched endlessly in both directions, a silent sentinel dividing two worlds. As we passed through it, my chest tightened with the weight of what we were about to face. The terrain was unrecognizable—shattered buildings, jagged metal, and debris scattered across the ground. The faint scent of the sea lingered in the air, strange and out of place amidst the chaos.

The explosions around us were relentless, louder, and closer with every step. The flashes of light made it feel as though the night itself was splintering apart. I gripped my machine gun tightly, its weight a constant reminder of the responsibility I carried. My back ached from the heavy bag strapped to me, the straps cutting into my shoulders with each step. My mag felt like a lead weight pulling me down, but there was no room for hesitation.

I glanced at my friends, their faces illuminated briefly by the bursts of light. They looked tired—drained in every sense of the word. Their movements were automatic, as if their bodies were on autopilot, driven by muscle memory and sheer determination.

THE FIRST ENCOUNTER

The deeper we moved into Gaza, the more hostile the terrain became. Broken buildings rose like jagged monuments to destruction, their crumbling walls casting long shadows in the dim light. The air smelled of smoke and scorched earth, a bitter reminder of what lay ahead.

Suddenly, we spotted a small structure still standing amidst the ruins. One of the commanders halted the formation. There was movement inside—a flashlight beam flickering for just a moment, and then, gunfire erupted.

"Face that way and guard!" my commander shouted, snapping me into action. I dropped to the ground, swinging my machine gun around to cover our rear. My role as the gunner was clear: protect the unit from any threat coming from behind. The tension was suffocating, every sound amplified by the adrenaline coursing through my veins.

The tanks reacted quickly, engaging the threat, but the tension never left. We regrouped quickly, checking for injuries and resetting our formation. The silence that followed was deafening, broken only by the crunch of rubble underfoot as we pressed on.

REFLECTIONS IN THE CHAOS

During a brief moment of stillness, my mind wandered. I thought about the life I had lived up to this point—the people I had met, the experiences that shaped me, and the dreams I still held onto. These memories brought a sense of calm, a flicker of strength amidst the chaos.

I also thought about our commander's clear instructions when we had just started out. We were here for a purpose, and that purpose was clear: to bring the hostages home and protect each other. The responsibility weighed heavily, but it also gave us direction. We weren't just soldiers; we were a team, a family, and each step forward was a testament to that bond.

SURVIVAL IN THE SAND

31/10/23

"We're staying in a ditch filled with sand, and the grains have found their way into everything—our clothes, our boots, even our skin. The itching is unbearable, but there's nothing we can do about it. I keep asking myself the same questions: When will this end? When will we complete our mission? The only thought that keeps me going is the idea of reuniting with my family. Their faces, their voices—it's all I can think about. Today, we got tuna and bread for both lunch and dinner. It's not much, but it's enough to keep us going. I keep repeating to myself, everything will be fine. It's not about comfort anymore; it's about survival."

The notebook was becoming my anchor. Every time I wrote in it, I felt like I was releasing a small piece of the overwhelming emotions I was carrying. By the time I wrote my entry on the second day in Gaza, the exhaustion had set in deep. My back ached from days of carrying my heavy bag and machine gun, my shoulders were raw from the straps digging into them, and my body was covered in sand.

The ditch where we had set up for the night was no better than the rest of the terrain. The sand seemed to find its way into everything: our boots, our uniforms, even the small cracks in our gear. It stuck to our skin, mixing with sweat and leaving us itchy and uncomfortable. The ditch offered little in terms of protection, but it was enough to keep us somewhat hidden and out of direct line of fire.

The monotony of waiting was brutal. Time felt warped in that sandy trench. Minutes stretched into hours, and the hours felt endless. The only markers of the passing time were the meals we were given—tuna and bread, the same thing for both lunch and dinner. It wasn't enough to fill us up, but it was enough to keep us going.

I stared at the small can of tuna in my hand, trying to focus on the act of eating, on something simple, just to distract myself from the questions running through my mind. *When will this end? When will we complete our mission? When will I get to go home?* These thoughts consumed me, circling endlessly in my head. The uncertainty was the hardest part, never knowing what was coming next or how long we'd be there.

THE POWER OF HOPE

Despite everything, I kept telling myself that everything would be fine. I didn't know if I truly believed it, but I needed to hold onto that hope. Hope was the only thing that could cut through the fear and discomfort. I thought of my family constantly, imagining their faces, their voices, their laughter. The thought of reuniting with them gave me strength.

The sand, the hunger, the noise, all of it faded a little when I thought about sitting with my family at the Shabbat table again, hearing my younger siblings argue playfully over who would get the last slice of challah. I imagined my parents' hugs, warm and grounding, the kind of hugs that make everything feel okay, no matter what. These memories became my refuge, my escape from the harsh reality around me.

THE REALITY OF WAR

As the day wore on, the reality of our situation remained unchanged. We were still in the ditch, still itchy from the sand, still watching and waiting for whatever came next. The sounds of war continued in the distance—explosions, gunfire, the occasional drone overhead.

Looking around at my brothers in the unit, I saw the same fatigue mirrored in their faces. The bags under their eyes, the slow movements, the way they sat hunched over their gear. We were all feeling it—the physical toll, the mental strain, and the unrelenting tension of being in a war zone.

FINDING LIGHT IN
THE DARKNESS

1/11/23

"I just flipped back and reread my last entry. Honestly, I need to shift my mindset and focus on the positives. Slowly but surely, I'm starting to adapt to this environment. It's not easy, but it's happening. I'm also building new friendships with the soldiers in my unit, which makes things a little lighter in such a heavy situation. Sometimes I catch myself smiling, imagining the moment I set foot back into Israel. How will it feel? The days feel slow—each one weighed down by the challenges we're facing—but I remind myself that every day brings us closer to the mission's end. One step at a time."

The morning of November 1 felt like a turning point. As I flipped back through my notebook and reread the words I had written over the past few days, I realized how heavy they were, filled with uncertainty and the weight of survival. It wasn't that those feelings had disappeared—far from it—but something inside me shifted. I made a choice: to focus on what little light I could find in the darkness.

ADAPTING TO THE ENVIRONMENT

By now, I had started to adjust to the harsh reality. The sand was still everywhere—stuck to our skin, our clothes, and even the inside of our gear—but I had grown used to it. The loud explosions and the constant hum of activity no longer bothered me the way they did on the first day. Instead, they became part of the background, a rhythm of war that I had unconsciously learned to live with.

Even the trench, which had felt like a miserable prison of dirt and discomfort, started to feel less oppressive. It wasn't home, but it was ours—a place where we found shelter, shared stories, and made the best of what we had.

NEW BONDS

One of the biggest changes was the friendships I was starting to form with the other soldiers in my unit. Maybe it was the simple fact that we all knew we had to rely on each other to make it through. Whatever it was, those bonds were forming quickly, and they felt real. There was a quiet comfort in knowing that I wasn't alone, that the soldiers beside me were facing the same struggles, the same fears. We didn't have to say much; a nod, a smile, or a shared look of understanding was often enough.

UNDER THE COVER

2/11/23

"4:00 AM – Enemy drones are flying overhead. Do they see us? It's impossible to tell in the pitch dark, except for the brief flashes of green and red lights that vanish just as quickly as they appear. We duck low, waiting for the tanks, snipers, and other soldiers to shoot them down. I slip on my night vision goggles, trying to spot the drones in the sky, but after a tense wait, the danger passes. No more drones.

17:00 – We received new intelligence: terrorists are approaching. The entire unit shifts into action as we prepare for their arrival. Two cars, 800 meters out. When the moment comes, I fire my mag, focusing on the second car. The shots land just before it enters a closed vision area, one that would've made it hard to track where they were heading. My focus sharpens as the bullets hit their mark."

THE TENSION IN THE AIR

The early hours of November 2nd began with a thick blanket of darkness. At 04:00, the silence was broken by the faint, unmistakable hum of enemy drones. Sent by Hamas, these drones were a constant threat, and their presence instantly set us on edge.

Their green and red lights flashed briefly before vanishing into the night, making them difficult to track. Just when you thought they were gone, they'd reappear in a completely different part of the sky, keeping us guessing and forcing us to stay alert. The sound of gunfire erupted around me as our snipers and tanks tried to take them down, their bursts of fire cutting through the darkness.

Tracking them was almost impossible at night. The vast black sky seemed to swallow them whole, their lights too faint to follow for more than a few seconds. During the day, spotting them was easier—they stood out against the clear sky—but under the cover of night, they became ghosts, haunting the skies and keeping us on edge.

I adjusted my night vision goggles, scanning the horizon for any sign of movement. My heart pounded as the minutes stretched on, each second a reminder of how exposed we were. Were they watching us? Pinpointing our location? Were they armed and ready to strike?

The hum lingered for what felt like an eternity before gradually fading into the distance. When the sky finally went silent, a wave of cautious relief swept over us. The immediate danger had passed, but the tension in the air didn't leave. We all knew this wouldn't be the last time we'd face them.

THE BUILD-UP

The day crawled forward, every moment carrying the weight of anticipation. By late afternoon, the tension shifted as we received new intelligence. A report came in that terrorists were approaching, and the entire atmosphere around us changed.

We prepared quickly, double-checking our weapons and gear, moving with precision. The details of the report were clear: two cars were coming, their occupants likely armed, and they were 800 meters out.

As the seconds ticked by, I could feel the adrenaline coursing through my veins. My hands tightened around my machine gun, its weight a reassuring constant. I crouched low, steadying myself, for what was coming.

THE ENCOUNTER

When the cars finally appeared, they were faint shapes in the distance, blurred by the heat and dust. I locked my sights on the second car, watching its movements carefully. It was veering toward a closed vision area—a blind spot that would make tracking it nearly impossible if it got through.

The moment came in a rush. I pulled the trigger, firing my mag in a calculated burst. The shots landed, striking the second car just before it disappeared into the blind zone. Relief and focus collided as I registered the impact.

The air around us seemed to still for a moment, the echoes of the shots fading into the distance. But the mission wasn't over.

THE PATROL

Afterward, we moved into patrol formation, sweeping the area for additional threats. Every movement felt deliberate, every step careful. My machine gun was at the ready, its familiar weight a constant reminder of the responsibility I carried. The landscape around us was a patchwork of shadows and ruined structures. Each shadow, every dark corner, felt like it could hide a potential danger. The tension never let up. But we were used to this by now-always on edge, always prepared, always ready.

REFLECTION IN THE QUIET MOMENTS

By the time the day ended, weakness had settled into every muscle. Yet, as I sat down to catch my breath, the events of the day replayed in my mind. The drones, the cars, the burst of fire—it was all so fast, yet every moment felt etched into my memory.

In those quiet moments, I thought about how this mission wasn't just about surviving the day—it was about moving forward together, one step at a time. It was about trust, about knowing that each of us was doing our part, and about the unspoken bond we shared as a unit.

Even though the day had been filled with danger and uncertainty, I felt a strange sense of clarity. This was war-harsh, relentless, and unforgiving. But we faced it head-on, together, with steady resolve.

THE MEANING OF APPRECIATION

3/11/23

"During guarding duty, I found myself reflecting on what 'appreciation' truly means. I told my friend, 'People who have everything often don't realize it. Think about it, do you eat good food every day? Shower? Sleep on a bed? Change into clean clothes? Now imagine one week without any of those things: canned food, sleeping on an inch of foam, wearing the same clothes, no showers, living outside. Would you survive?' Out here, those basic comforts don't exist, and it changes how you see the world. The more you go without, the more you realize how much those small things mean."

GUARD DUTY CONVERSATIONS

The night stretched endlessly before us, broken only by the occasional sounds of distant gunfire and explosions. They were faint, yet sharp enough to remind us that the calm was a fragile illusion, a brief pause in the chaos. Guard duty wasn't just about scanning the horizon or watching for movement; it was also a time to think, to reflect, and sometimes, to talk.

I was stationed alongside one of my friends. Both of us sat quietly at first, our eyes scanning the darkness, our weapons ready. The silence between us felt natural, a shared understanding of the gravity of where we were. But as minutes turned into an hour, the conversation began—slowly at first, then evolving into one of those rare, honest exchanges that only seem to happen in places like this.

THE QUESTION OF APPRECIATION

A thought had been circling my mind since we entered Gaza, one that felt too important not to share. "Do you ever think about the meaning of appreciation?" I asked my friend Lev, breaking the silence.

He tilted his head slightly, curious but cautious. "What do you mean?"

I paused, trying to find the right words. "Back home, life was so different. We had everything we needed—good food, warm beds, clean clothes, showers—and we never thought twice about any of it. But out here? Every little thing feels … massive."

He nodded, encouraging me to continue, so I pressed on. "We're eating canned food, sleeping on an inch of foam, wearing the same clothes for days. Showers? Forget about it. And yet, somehow, we're surviving. But imagine someone who's used to having all of those things suddenly thrown into this life. Could they make it even a week?"

The thought lingered in the air between us. I could see the recognition in his eyes. It wasn't a criticism of anyone back home; it was an acknowledgment of how hardship strips life down to its raw essentials.

"People who have everything don't really know what everything is," I added, the words hanging heavy in the quiet night.

LEARNING FROM THE STRUGGLE

This wasn't about complaining—it was about gratitude. Hardship has a way of teaching you what truly matters. Back home, the basics—food, water, a warm bed—were just part of the routine, things so ordinary they were often overlooked. But here, those basics became treasures.

Every meal, no matter how simple, felt like a celebration. A few minutes to rest felt like a luxury. Even a small joke shared between soldiers was enough to lift the weight of the day, if only for a moment. Appreciation for us wasn't just about having more, but about recognizing the value of what we already have. Out here, stripped of all comforts, we began to understand the true worth of life's simplest gifts.

A QUIET REALIZATION

As our conversation faded, the night around us seemed quieter somehow. I found myself replaying the words I had just spoken, realizing how much my own perspective had shifted.

Back home, I'd had everything—a warm house, fresh meals, clean clothes, and the security of knowing I was safe. Yet I had barely stopped to think about how much those things mattered. Here, with all of that gone, every small comfort felt enormous.

I pulled out my notebook, the faint light of a distant flare illuminating the page. Writing had become my way of processing these thoughts, of grounding myself when the world felt too chaotic. This was a moment I didn't want to forget.

A GLIMPSE OF COMFORT

4/11/23

"Today I woke up with such a good feeling. I still don't understand why ... Maybe because we received more food and water, including a package of croissants that we divided within our unit. It was a very cold night, though, and we were woken up every two hours. Now it's 1:45 PM, and I'm sitting in the tent. Most of the soldiers are sleeping. I don't know why, but it's hard for me to sleep during the day. I have this specific feeling that I have to be aware of what is going on every second. I prefer to sleep during the night when I get the chance to."

A MORNING OF GRATITUDE

When I woke up that morning, something felt different. It wasn't peace—far from it. We were still deep in Gaza, surrounded by the tension of war, but there was a subtle sense of comfort in the air. Maybe it was the little things, like the extra food and water we'd received. In a place where survival depended on the barest necessities, even the smallest blessings felt monumental.

The croissants were an unexpected treat, something so out of place in the grim environment that they seemed almost magical. They weren't fresh or flaky, but that didn't matter. Just having something sweet, something that reminded us of life outside, was enough to lift our spirits.

When we realized there wasn't enough for everyone, we didn't hesitate. Without a word, we began splitting them in half with our bare hands, ensuring that every soldier got a piece. The gesture was simple, but it spoke volumes about the bond we shared. I can still remember the taste—the soft sweetness of the chocolate, the hint of sugar that seemed to melt on my tongue. For a brief moment, I forgot about the discomfort and the danger. That little piece of croissant brought a smile to my face, a rare moment of joy amidst the chaos.

THE COLD OF THE NIGHT

The night before had been unforgiving. Without tents for shelter, we slept under the open sky, exposed to the biting chill of the night. The hard sand beneath us grew damp and icy as the hours passed, seeping through our uniforms and leaving us shivering.

Taking off our boots, vests, or helmets wasn't an option. The constant threat of enemy fire kept us on high alert, even in moments of supposed rest. My bulletproof vest, with its heavy plates, made lying flat almost impossible. I could only manage to sleep on my side, the hard surface pressing uncomfortably against my ribs.

My machine gun was my constant companion. I kept it close, the magazine loaded, my hand resting on the handle even as I tried to sleep. It wasn't just a precaution—it was a necessity. The knowledge that I could wake up at any moment to danger kept me prepared, ready to act in an instant.

It wasn't the kind of rest that left you feeling refreshed. It was survival sleep, shallow and fragmented, interrupted by the slightest sound or movement. I understood, deep down, that this was my reality now. There was no use wishing for a comfortable bed or a warm blanket. This was war, and the only way through was to adapt.

A RESTLESS AFTERNOON

By the time afternoon came, most of the unit had collapsed into a much-needed sleep. Soldiers were sprawled across the sand, their helmets tilted over their faces or their arms crossed tightly against the cold. The soft murmurs of sleep filled the air, broken only by the occasional sound of someone shifting position.

But I couldn't bring myself to join them. Exhaustion weighed heavily on me, but something inside refused to let me rest. It wasn't fear, exactly. It was a sense of responsibility, an unshakable feeling that I needed to stay alert. I sat quietly, my eyes scanning the horizon, listening to the faint hum of activity around me.

Even as I watched my brothers rest, I thought about how much I preferred the nights. There was something about the cover of darkness that felt safer, despite the dangers. The night offered a routine, a signal to rest, even if only for a few hours.

Daytime was different. The light brought clarity, and with clarity came vulnerability. Every movement felt exposed, every sound seemed amplified. Yet, even in the quiet of the afternoon, I couldn't shake the feeling that something could happen at any moment.

A NEW MISSION

5/11/23

"Today, I woke up on guard duty and watched the sunrise—a brief moment of peace before the day began. We received a new mission: tomorrow, we'll be moving the entire unit and our supplies 2 kilometers deeper into Gaza. It doesn't sound like much, but with the weight of bullets, gear, and supplies on our backs, every step feels like a challenge. We spent the day organizing and preparing, double-checking every detail to ensure we were ready. I've already started drinking extra water, knowing how important it is to stay hydrated for the journey ahead. As I sit here, all I can think is, 'If I did it once, I can do it again.'"

PREPARING FOR THE NEXT STEP

The sunrise that morning was unlike any I'd seen before—its golden rays piercing through the stark landscape of Gaza, bathing the barren terrain in a deceptive warmth. I was on guard duty, my machine gun resting at my side, as I stood watch over a world that felt both haunting and surreal. For a moment, I allowed myself to take it in, to appreciate the rare calm of the morning. Moments like these didn't come often.

Not long after, the calm was interrupted by the announcement of our next mission. The orders were clear: tomorrow, we'd be moving the entire unit and our supplies two kilometers deeper into Gaza. Two kilometers—it didn't sound like much. Back home, it was a quick jog around the block or a walk to the store. But here, in this place, two kilometers was a world away.

It wasn't just the distance; it was the weight. Every soldier carried what felt like a small mountain strapped to their back. Bullets, weapons, supplies—every ounce mattered, and every ounce added to the strain. The thought of moving all of it again, step by grueling step, filled the air with a collective understanding of what lay ahead.

THE RITUAL OF PREPARATION

When a new mission was announced, it was more than just a change of plans—it was a signal for us to begin the meticulous ritual of preparation. Every detail mattered. We couldn't afford to leave anything behind, whether it was gear, supplies, or even the smallest trace of our presence.

As a unit, we moved with purpose. Gear was checked and rechecked. Supplies were divided and redistributed, ensuring every soldier carried their share. The weight on our shoulders was literal, but the responsibility felt even heavier.

Then came the cleanup—a part of every mission that felt as important as the preparation itself. We swept the area, picking up any trace that might reveal we had been there. Food wrappers, empty water bottles, even scuffs in the dirt—we left nothing behind. The goal was simple: make it look like we had never been there.

The process was grueling, especially under the harsh Gaza sun. The sand clung to us as we worked, finding its way into our boots, our clothes, even our gear. But we pushed through, knowing the importance of the task.

MENTAL AND PHYSICAL PREPARATION

As we prepared, I focused on staying hydrated, sipping water throughout the day to ready myself for the trek. In this environment, dehydration was an enemy we couldn't afford to ignore. Every drop mattered.

Despite the physical preparation, the mental battle was just as real. I couldn't help but think about the journey ahead, about the weight I'd be carrying and the unknowns waiting for us two kilometers deeper into Gaza. But I reminded myself: I've done this before, and I'll do it again.

THE UNSPOKEN BOND

During times like these, the bond within our unit grew stronger. We worked in silence for the most part, each soldier focused on their tasks, but there was an unspoken understanding that tied us together. A nod, a pat on the back, or a quick shared glance was enough to convey what words couldn't.

As the sun began to set, we finished our preparations. The area was spotless, our gear was packed, and the plan was clear. Tomorrow, we'd take another step forward, another step deeper into the unknown.

For now, I allowed myself to rest, even if only for a moment. I lay back on the hard ground, my gear beside me, and stared up at the darkening sky. My body ached, my mind raced, but somewhere beneath it all, there was a quiet determination. This was what we trained for, what we prepared for.

DAVID AND THE DRONE

6/11/23

"This morning, I shared a can of tuna with David. He's 54, long past the age when reserves are mandatory, but he chose to be here because he felt he couldn't sit back after everything that happened. David serves in a special intelligence reserve unit, responsible for gathering field information and supporting counter-terror efforts. His dedication is something I deeply admire. We packed our bags, cleaned up, and started the long walk—two kilometers to find a solid building where we could finally settle down. But about 1.5 kilometers in, I heard the sharp buzz of a drone overhead. I looked up, and there it was—an enemy drone hovering 200 meters above us. Orders flew out to duck, and snipers fired quickly, taking it down. As I hit the ground and began praying, a strange calm washed over me. I accepted the life I was living and the fragility of this moment. If this was my destiny, so be it."

BREAKFAST WITH DAVID

That morning began like so many others in Gaza—early. I woke up, stretched my aching shoulders, and sat down to share a simple meal of tuna with David, a man who had quickly earned my respect.

David was 54 years old, much older than the rest of us. At his age, he didn't have to be here—he wasn't obligated to serve in the reserves. Yet here he was, dressed in uniform, sitting in the dirt with me as if he were decades younger. There was something remarkable about him. His heart, his drive—it was stronger than many of the young soldiers I knew.

As we ate, he began to share his story. He told me that he had a daughter at home, a young girl who was his entire world. "She didn't want me to come," he admitted, his voice steady, his eyes gazing into the distance. "But after 7 October, I couldn't stay back. There was no way I could sit at home and watch you boys head to the frontlines while I did nothing."

I listened intently, struck by his resolve. It wasn't easy for a man of his age to pick up his gear, leave his family, and step into war. "I wanted to come with you," he continued. "To stand alongside you. To make sure I was doing my part."

There was no ego in his words—no bravado. Just pure conviction. I could see the fire in his eyes, the kind of fire that only comes from knowing you're doing the right thing, no matter how hard it is. Talking to him reminded me why we were all here: to protect, to fight, and to stand together.

We spoke for the rest of the morning, sharing stories, thoughts, and a quiet camaraderie that can only form in moments like this. He gave me strength without even realizing it. I looked at him and thought, *If he can be here, at his age, leaving behind the family he loves, then I can do this, too.*

When it was time to pack up and move on, I shook his hand—firm and quiet, like two people who understood more than they said out loud. He climbed into a Hummer and drove off. He didn't say where he was going, and I didn't ask. Maybe it was classified, or maybe he just didn't want to say. Part of me thought he didn't know either. That was the last time I saw him. I was just grateful we had that moment—two soldiers, two strangers, sharing something real in the middle of war. In a place where everything felt temporary, that small connection gave me something to hold on to.

THE DRONE

The day moved on, and we started our march to a new location—another 2 kilometers deeper into Gaza. Each step was heavy, the weight of my gear and machine gun digging into me. The sand was relentless, slipping into every part of my uniform and sticking to my sweat-soaked skin.

At about 1.5 kilometers in, everything changed.

I heard it before I saw it—the faint, unmistakable zzzzz sound above us. My heart sank as I instinctively looked up, scanning the sky. And there it was—hovering about 200 meters above me. An enemy drone.

For a split second, no one moved. It was hard to tell what kind of drone it was. Hamas sent different types—some with cameras for reconnaissance, some with explosives, and others capable of firing directly at us. The uncertainty made it even more terrifying. We didn't know if it was watching us, ready to explode, or preparing to attack.

Then, chaos erupted.

Shots rang out from the snipers as well as the drone, loud and sharp, breaking the tense silence. "Duck!" someone yelled. I didn't need to be told twice. My instincts kicked in, and I dropped to the ground, my heart pounding against my chest. The weight of my gear pressed me into the dirt, but I didn't care. My eyes locked on the drone as it hovered, its green and red lights flashing against the bright sky.

The drone was always there, clear against the blue sky, but it moved so fast it seemed to jump from one point to another. Daylight made it easier to see, though not any easier to predict.

In that moment, lying face down in the sand, I whispered the words that had been passed down through generations of Jews facing moments of fear and uncertainty: *"Shema Yisrael, Adonai Eloheinu, Adonai Echad."* A declaration of faith that translates to: *"Hear, O Israel, the Lord is our God, the Lord is One."*

The *Shema Yisrael* is one of the most sacred prayers in Judaism. It's often the last prayer uttered in times of danger, a plea for protection and a moment of connection with something greater than yourself.

I prayed with everything in me, accepting whatever would come next. In those few seconds, my mind slowed, and a strange calm settled over me. If this was my destiny, then so be it.

The drone wavered, as if it couldn't decide its next move. Then, a final round of shots rang out, and I heard an explosion—Boom. The snipers had hit their mark. The drone was down.

THE AFTERMATH

I exhaled deeply, realizing I'd been holding my breath the entire time. Around me, the other soldiers started to rise, brushing the sand from their uniforms, their faces still pale. As we resumed our march, I couldn't stop thinking about David's determination, his courage, and the way he stood alongside us as if he were one of the youngest men in the unit. If he could face this at his age, then so could I. I adjusted the straps of my heavy bag, gripped my machine gun a little tighter, and kept walking. There was no room for fear. Not now. Not with so much at stake. In war, you learn quickly that strength doesn't always come from physical power. It comes from moments like these—from the prayers you whisper in the dark, from the people you draw inspiration from, and from the quiet resolve to keep moving forward no matter what.

THE GROUND BENEATH US

7/11/23

"2.5 km deeper into Gaza, it can't get any darker at this point. We walk at a fast pace in order to reach the location as safely as possible. There is no view towards the ground; we are constantly walking on big rocks and pieces of metal due to the destruction. One of my commanders loses sight of the soldiers that were leading us. At this moment, we do a 360-degree formation and wait for the captain to find us. We finally reached the other crew and arrived at a building that we suspected had mines inside, so we couldn't enter until it was cleared. We find a house at about 3:30 AM, and we get straight to cleaning as well as preparing the guarding stands, also placing spots for bathroom waste and sleep. I did not sleep at all that night, but I'm feeling strong."

THE DARKNESS OF THE DEEP

As we pushed 2.5 kilometers deeper into Gaza, the landscape grew heavier—the air felt thick, the silence oppressive, even the darkness seemed to press in on us. The streets we followed were uneven, choked with twisted metal, broken concrete, and abandoned belongings.

Every step demanded attention. The ground beneath us was cracked and uneven, sometimes giving way under our boots. I could feel the tremor of distant explosions in my chest, each one a reminder that danger could erupt at any moment. Above us, the sky was a muted slate, illuminated only by the occasional tracer round streaking across the gloom.

MOVING FORWARD

Our mission was clear: keep moving, stay together, and reach the next location as safely and quickly as possible. The urgency in our formation was tangible. We moved in near silence, our eyes darting between the shadows, our fingers brushing the triggers of our weapons.

One of our commanders led the way, his presence steadying us. But even the most experienced among us weren't immune to the chaos of war. Somewhere along the way, we lost sight of the soldiers at the front of the formation.

The unit froze, and the air felt electric with tension.

A 360-DEGREE FORMATION

Immediately, we dropped into a defensive 360-degree formation, our instinct and training taking over. Each of us locked into position, covering a different angle, creating a protective circle. Every sound became amplified—the crunch of debris under someone's boot, the faint hum of a drone, the distant echoes of explosions.

I knelt in position, my heart pounding in my chest. Time felt suspended, every second stretching into an eternity. I scanned the darkness, searching for any sign of movement, my weapon ready.

Minutes passed, though it felt much longer, until the captain found us and regrouped the unit. The tension broke just enough for us to breathe, but we knew we had to move quickly to make up for lost time.

A BUILDING TOO DANGEROUS

When we finally reached the location, relief was short-lived. The building we were supposed to secure was suspected to have mines inside, although it wasn't confirmed. This made it impossible to enter safely. The realization hit hard—we were exhausted, desperate for shelter, and now forced to find another option.

After a short search, we located a smaller house nearby, reaching it at around 3:30 AM. It wasn't ideal, but it was something.

PREPARING FOR THE NIGHT

The moment we entered, the work began. There was no time to rest. We cleaned the space, cleared debris, and set up guarding posts to secure the area. Every task felt vital: designating spots for bathroom waste, organizing sleeping arrangements, and making sure the house was defensible.

We were starting to feel very tired, but we pushed through, each of us driven by the knowledge that we had no other choice. This was survival, plain and simple.

Despite our efforts to make the house as livable as possible, sleep was out of the question for me. The tension of the day lingered, keeping me alert. My body begged for rest, but my mind refused to let go of the awareness that danger was always close.

PART TWO
THE JOURNAL

8/11/23

"12:24 PM — We've reached Gaza City. Each day, we move deeper and sleep in different bombed-out buildings. Engineers check every structure to ensure it's safe for us to stay. Last night, we slept in a penthouse. It was completely destroyed, but I could still see hints of the life the family who lived there once had—a pool, jacuzzi, a rooftop overlooking the beach, even a theater. The constant shifts in temperature are starting to affect us. It gets hot during the day and cold at night, and my MAG 2, who helps carry some of my gear, isn't feeling well. I've been doing my best to help him stay on his feet because his load is also mine to bear.

Supporting him, and the others, gives me strength too—it reminds me we're all in this together, pushing forward step by step."

REACHING GAZA CITY

By midday, we had reached Gaza City, a sprawling urban center that had once thrived with families, businesses, and the rhythms of daily life. Now, it was a ghost town. The streets were eerily quiet.

Every day, we moved deeper into the city, further into the heart of destruction, and every night, we searched for a place to rest. These weren't homes anymore; they were remnants, hollow shells of what they used to be. The engineers in our unit became essential, carefully assessing each building to determine if it was structurally safe enough to use as shelter.

THE PENTHOUSE

One night, we came across a building that stood out—a penthouse apartment. Even in its destroyed state, you could tell it had once been a place of incredible luxury. The rooftop terrace overlooked the city and the sea beyond. There was a pool, a jacuzzi, a home theater, and a pool table, amenities that told the story of a life lived in privilege.

Walking through the rubble, I couldn't help but feel the weight of the contrast. Whoever had lived here had been living a dream life—right on the beach, surrounded by comfort and excess. Now, it was a crumbled ruin, like everything else around us. It was a stark reminder of how quickly life can change, how even the most secure and comfortable realities can be destroyed in an instant.

THE WEIGHT OF RESPONSIBILITY

By this point, my role as a machine gunner had become second nature, but that didn't make it any easier than the first day. From the moment I was assigned the responsibility of the MAG, I knew the weight wasn't just physical—it was mental, emotional, and deeply tied to the safety of my unit.

When I was first given the gun, another soldier in the unit, who had experience with it, stepped forward. Although he was assigned to a different task, he stayed by my side during those early days of preparation. "You're MAG 1 now," he told me with a steady voice, explaining the role.

He would be my MAG 2, my second-in-command, supporting me in every way possible. If the gun jammed, he'd help fix it. If I needed to reload under pressure, he'd be there. And if the worst happened to me, he'd take over. We worked as a team, our roles bound by mutual trust.

But as the days wore on, his health began to decline. One morning, I watched in horror as he suddenly leaned over and began coughing up blood. "I can't continue," he said softly, his voice heavy with regret.

He unstrapped his heavy bag, which carried part of my ammunition, and handed it to me. That simple act felt monumental. I understood what it meant: I'd be carrying the full burden of the MAG from that moment forward.

THE PHYSICAL TOLL

I tried to distribute the extra ammunition among the other soldiers in the unit, asking if anyone had space in their bags. Most of them were already carrying their own full loads—food, water, ammunition, and gear—but one soldier managed to squeeze a few rounds into his pack.

The rest I had to carry myself. I stuffed the remaining bullets into my already overloaded bag, tightening the straps and bracing myself for what was to come. The MAG hung in front of me, its weight pressing into my chest, while my back bore the strain of the ammunition and gear. Every step felt like a battle.

When we moved, I struggled to keep up. Running was the hardest part—not just because I was carrying so much weight, but because I had to match the pace of soldiers who weren't nearly as encumbered. At times, it felt like the straps of my gear were squeezing the air out of me, but I pushed through. I had no choice.

HELPING MY MAG 2

Before my MAG 2 left, I did everything I could to support him. He was struggling under the weight of his gear, the long days of walking, and the heat that bore down on us relentlessly. I encouraged him to hydrate, to eat, to rest when he could.

Helping him gave me purpose, even as I carried my own burdens. There's something about focusing on someone else that takes your mind off your own struggles. Supporting him reminded me why we were out here—not just to complete our mission, but to protect and look out for one another.

When he finally had to leave, I understood that it wasn't weakness—it was necessity. Still, it felt like a piece of my own strength was walking away with him.

SEARCHING
THE SHADOWS

9/11/23

"10:18 – We prepared to search for tunnels after receiving classified info about their exact locations. Our task was to confirm the sites so they could be demolished.

13:24 – Back from the mission. We found one tunnel and a makeshift bomb. The adrenaline was intense as we left, knowing it could explode any second. About 300 meters away, the bomb went off, the loudest explosion I've ever heard. The sky went dark with smoke. Later, we searched again, this time for weapons. By evening, we had uncovered flags of Hamas and the Islamic Jihad and a bag full of weapons, including a machine gun. Tanks arrived with fresh supplies, food, and ammunition to end the long day."

NOVEMBER 9, 2023 – TUNNEL HUNT

The morning started strangely quiet. In Gaza, that kind of silence always meant something was coming. At 10:18, the calm broke with a mission briefing. The commanders stood around a map, pointing to red circles and speaking in low, serious tones. Intelligence had confirmed something we all feared: Hamas tunnels were nearby—likely right under the ruined buildings we had seen the day before.

These tunnels weren't just holes in the ground. They were lifelines for the enemy, used to move fighters, smuggle weapons, and maybe even hide hostages. If we didn't find and mark them, other units—or worse, civilians—could pay the price. Missing one wasn't an option.

Twenty of us were chosen. I was assigned to the back of the formation as the machine gunner, my responsibility clear: protect the rear. My back was already sore from carrying the weapon day after day, but this was no time to focus on pain. The moment we stepped out, everything had to be about the mission.

Before we reached the main building, we made sure the entire area around it was clear. The commanders were sharp, scanning every alley and rooftop. My own commander sprinted up to me several times, pointing to suspicious areas—shattered windows, twisted corners of walls—ordering me to fire. I pressed my shoulder into the stock and fired long, controlled bursts, the sound crashing through the air like thunder. My body rattled with each shot, but the adrenaline dulled everything else.

We moved slowly toward the building. It looked like a ghost had swallowed it whole—dark, crumbling, and silent. Dust hung in the air like fog. Each soldier stepped lightly, rifles up, hearts pounding. Inside, broken furniture was scattered across the floor, and the smell of wet concrete and something metallic filled the space.

Suddenly, a loud voice cracked through the tension: "Bomb! Bomb! Everyone out now!"

No one hesitated. Boots scrambled across broken tiles. One soldier tripped and nearly went down—I grabbed his vest and pulled him up. I stayed at the rear, making sure no one was left behind. Then I ran.

We were about 300 meters away when the building behind us exploded. The blast was huge—louder than anything I had ever heard. It shook the ground like an earthquake. A massive cloud of black smoke rose into the air, and chunks of the building flew out like they were weightless.

The shockwave hit us hard. I could feel the heat on the back of my neck even from that distance. My ears rang, my body shook, and my hands trembled around the machine gun. But we were alive.

We found out later that a special engineering team had safely detonated the bomb after confirming we were clear. They're among the IDF's most skilled professionals—experts in handling explosives and underground threats. Their job is to face the danger so others don't have to. Knowing they were involved made it clear this mission was far from routine.

A STRATEGIC VICTORY

After the blast, we sat down in a semi-circle to catch our breath. Our commander said something that stuck with me: "You all followed the plan, and because of that, you made it out."

That hit hard. If we had rushed in or skipped a step while clearing the area, the outcome could have been very different. It's possible we scared off whoever was watching, or we took out a fighter before he could trigger the bomb. Either way, our caution and teamwork had saved lives.

We weren't just checking buildings—we were stopping future attacks before they could happen. And for the first time that day,

I felt a deep sense of pride. We had done something important. We had made it back.

SHABBAT

10/11/23

"*It's 09:55. We evacuated to a new building this morning, leaving behind an area that was too dangerous because of the explosives nearby. Now, we're deep in the Hamas zone, surrounded by reminders of the conflict—flags and symbols of their presence are everywhere. Today is Shabbat, and while the day carries its own significance, I can't help but hope this will be the last one I spend in Gaza. I long for the moment I can step out of here, holding the Israeli flag high and steady, my machine gun resting firmly on my shoulder. That image gives me hope.*"

A NEW BUILDING

The morning began with urgency. At 09:55, orders came in: we had to evacuate. The area where we had been stationed was no longer safe—explosives had been detected nearby. This wasn't the first time we'd had to leave a building on short notice, but the tension of these moments never eased.

We packed quickly, gathering our gear and leaving behind any trace that we had been there. Every step toward the new location carried the weight of uncertainty. The building we moved into was deep in the Hamas zone, surrounded by a stark reminder of the conflict we were entrenched in.

SIGNS OF THE ENEMY

Inside, the walls were covered with Hamas flags, their symbols a glaring presence against the broken concrete. Seeing them up close was unsettling—not just markers of the enemy but also reminders of the destruction we were working to end.

As we secured the building, I found myself reflecting on the sharp contrast between this place and the homes I had left behind in Israel. Here, the walls seemed to echo with tension, carrying the shadows of violence and fear. Back home, those walls would hold family photographs, laughter, and life.

SHABBAT IN GAZA

It was Shabbat—a day meant for rest and gratitude, but in Gaza, it felt anything but restful. Still, we took a moment to gather together. It wasn't much: a small blessing over the food we had, shared with quiet reverence. Despite the chaos around us, it felt important to acknowledge the day, to be thankful for even the smallest things.

The simplicity of the meal—whatever rations we had—didn't diminish the meaning of the blessing. Saying it as a group gave us a fleeting sense of unity, a brief moment where we could feel connected to something beyond the war.

THE QUESTIONS OF WAR

11/11/23

"Since the war began, I keep asking myself: Why do bad things happen to good people? Why did three of my closest friends lose their lives? Was it their destiny? War gives you too much time to think—most of it spent battling your own mind rather than the enemy outside. The harsh reality is that none of us truly understands what's happening. We only get bits of information about our next mission or the enemy's movements. What's going on back home? We have no idea. All we know is that this is our first war, and we pray it's our last. I hold onto the hope of living a life filled with happiness and health."

THE WEIGHT OF THE QUESTIONS

War forces you to confront questions you'd rather avoid, ones that linger in the silence between the chaos. The question that haunted me the most was simple yet impossible to answer: Why do bad things happen to good people?

I couldn't stop thinking about my three friends who had been killed. Their faces appeared in my mind often—smiling, laughing, full of life. They weren't just soldiers; they were good people, the kind who lifted others up, who made everything feel a little lighter even in the darkest moments. And now, they were gone.

Was it destiny? Fate? Or just the random cruelty of war? The more I asked myself, the more elusive the answers became. In war, you learn to live with uncertainty because you have no other choice.

THE BATTLE WITHIN

The real battle wasn't always the one outside. It wasn't the sound of gunfire or the rumble of explosions—it was the war raging inside my own mind. The grief, the fear, the doubts—all of it sat with me, waiting for the quiet moments to rise to the surface.

We had plenty of quiet in between missions, long stretches of waiting that stretched endlessly. And with the waiting came the questions, the unshakable thoughts that gnawed at me.

The hardest part wasn't the physical weakness or even the danger—it was the mental toll. We were fed only fragments of information: where we'd go next, what the enemy was doing. Beyond that, we were left in the dark.

Back home felt like a different world, one we were cut off from entirely. Was my family safe? What were they thinking? Did they know where I was, what I was going through? We didn't know. And not knowing made the isolation unbearable.

A CLEAR VISION

None of us entered Gaza for ourselves. None of us fought for personal gain or glory. We stepped into this war with the clear vision of what we were protecting behind us: our families, our friends, our homes. That understanding was what gave us value and purpose.

We weren't here for destruction—we were here for protection. Our mission was to safeguard the lives we loved, the ones waiting for us beyond the border. And in that purpose, I found strength.

THE CHAOTIC NIGHT

12/11/23

"It's currently 8:38 AM. Last night was chaotic. It was about 11:45 PM when I was about to close my eyes, when all of a sudden, we came under fire from Hamas. Every night, we set up guardian posts all around the building, including the outside entrance, which is 'lively.' Last night, the outside post got hit, and we were all alerted as the shots rang out. Everyone got up, and without wasting time, we loaded our weapons and waited for new updates. I prepared my magazines with 150 bullets each—600 in total—and made sure my machine gun was ready. We waited a couple of hours as the area got cleared up by a special unit. We then climbed our way to the third floor of the building to scan the area from above. We suspect that a terrorist exited from one of the tunnels, exchanged fire, and then returned. Nobody was hurt. At 6:00 AM, we walked 1.5 km deeper into Gaza City, where I am at this moment. We received a new mission, which is *that we will be guarding a supply strip from the top floor of an abandoned hotel so that the top elite units can deploy their units underground to see if there are any hostages. We are really close to the location of the hotel, and as I look up into the sky, I see five military drones that are following us at all times, scanning the area so that we are safe."*

THE HOTEL AND THE CHAOS BEFORE DAWN

The night began like many others—a mix of fatigue and vigilance. By 11:45 PM, I was ready to finally close my eyes and rest. The relentless days and long nights had left me drained, and my body craved sleep. But just as I began to drift off, the sharp sound of gunfire shattered the stillness.

The outside guardian post had been hit. This wasn't entirely unexpected; the entrance to the building was always the most exposed and unpredictable area. It was the "lively" spot where threats seemed to materialize out of nowhere.

INSTANT READINESS

The response was immediate. Adrenaline surged as every soldier shot to their feet, weapons loaded and ready. It was automatic now—no hesitation, no second-guessing. I grabbed my machine gun, hands moving swiftly to prepare four magazines, each holding 150 bullets. That gave me 600 rounds, enough to face whatever might come.

We all stood at the ready, waiting for instructions, our breaths heavy in the thick tension. This wasn't fear; it was focus. Every sound outside, every faint echo, was amplified in the silence as we braced for the unknown.

Special units were deployed to sweep the area, and we waited in a state of heightened alert. Time stretched on, every second heavy with the possibility of action.

SCANNING THE CITY

Hours passed before the all-clear came through. No one was hurt, but the story of the night began to take shape. We learned that a terrorist had likely emerged from one of the many underground tunnels, engaged the outside post, and retreated back underground.

To ensure the area was secure, our unit moved to the third floor of the building. From this elevated vantage point, we scanned the surroundings. The city sprawled before us, its broken silhouette illuminated by faint flashes of distant gunfire and the occasional flare. The stillness of the moment felt eerie, like the calm before another inevitable storm.

MOVING DEEPER

At 6:00 AM, new orders came in. We were to move 1.5 kilometers deeper into Gaza City, to secure a supply strip from the top floor of an abandoned hotel. The mission wasn't just about securing the building; it was about providing cover for elite units preparing to descend underground in search of hostages.

The march to the hotel was both physically and mentally draining. Each step was a careful negotiation with the rubble-strewn streets. The city's destruction was everywhere—buildings reduced to skeletal remains, debris scattered like confetti at a grim parade.

THE HOTEL

When we finally reached the hotel, it stood as a stark reminder of the devastation around us. While much of it was damaged, parts of the structure still stood, offering a rare glimpse of something that hadn't been completely reduced to rubble.

We moved quickly to secure the top floor, navigating through the debris that cluttered every hallway and room. The weight of the mission pressed heavily on us. Every movement had to be deliberate, every decision precise. This wasn't just about securing a building—it was about ensuring the safety of those who might be relying on us from below, and protecting each other as we faced the unknown.

EYES IN THE SKY

As I took my position, I looked up and saw five military drones circling overhead. Their constant hum filled the air, a reminder that we weren't alone. The drones were our unseen allies, scanning the area for threats and providing an added layer of security.

They were a symbol of the balance we were trying to maintain—technology and humanity working together in the midst of chaos. Yet, even with their presence, the vulnerability remained.

THE CAPTURE

13/11/23

"7:30 AM – We were informed that our current location was a partially standing hotel where we would be stationed for the next week. Earlier, I witnessed the capture of a terrorist emerging from a nearby building. A special unit interrogated him and managed to extract valuable information—there were tunnels nearby, and Hamas was aware of our location. Shortly after, the explosives unit arrived and demolished several buildings around the area to neutralize any threats. At one point, I was assigned to guard the captured terrorist, ensuring he didn't remove his blindfold. It was a surreal moment, yet another reminder of the constant danger surrounding us."

CAPTURING SHADOWS

The morning felt heavy, the kind of weight that lingered in the air as if the day itself was warning us of what lay ahead. We had been informed that our new base of operations was a partially standing hotel—just enough of its structure remained intact to offer us cover. We were told we'd be stationed there for at least a week.

Shortly after sunrise, we received reports of suspicious activity in a nearby building. As tanks rumbled into position, scanning the area, one of the soldiers spotted a man emerging cautiously, his hands raised high in surrender. It was a Hamas operative, and a special reconnaissance team working alongside us immediately took him into custody.

THE CAPTURE

The scene felt almost surreal as the team led the captured man toward our temporary base. Known for their expertise in operating deep behind enemy lines, this specialized unit excelled in reconnaissance, sabotage, and identifying high-value targets. Watching them escort the man, there was no struggle—just the stark image of his raised hands framed against the rubble and destruction around us. Once at the base, he was handed over to the intelligence and interrogation specialists. Their mission was clear: to extract critical information that could save lives and reveal hidden threats.

I stayed close, observing as these elite soldiers worked quickly. Within hours, they had extracted vital information. The terrorist revealed that there were several tunnels in the area, hidden beneath the rubble, and, more chillingly, that Hamas knew exactly where we were stationed. The realization that our location was compromised added an extra layer of tension to an already fraught situation.

NEUTRALIZING THE THREAT

The explosives team wasted no time. They moved systematically, targeting and demolishing buildings close to the one where the terrorist had been hiding. Each detonation was a calculated strike, shaking the ground and sending plumes of smoke into the air. It was a clear message: we were here, and we weren't going anywhere.

GUARD DUTY

Later that night, I was assigned to guard the captured terrorist. The task was straightforward: ensure he didn't remove his blindfold and prevent any attempts at escape. But it was anything but simple.

In the quiet hours of the night, as the rest of the unit rested, I sat across from him. He was restless, constantly shifting and trying to tug at the fabric covering his eyes. Every so often, I had to remind him, firmly but calmly, to stop. His movements weren't aggressive, but they carried a tension that kept me on edge.

The stillness around us amplified every sound—the faint rustle of his movements, the distant hum of drones, and the occasional echo of a far-off explosion. My grip on my weapon was steady, my focus unwavering. This was my responsibility, and I wouldn't let my guard down.

A LONG NIGHT

The hours crawled by. I didn't let myself think too much about who he was or what he had done. It wasn't my place to judge—that would come later, handled by others. My job was clear: to ensure that he remained secure and that no harm came to my unit because of him.

As dawn broke, the sky began to shift from darkness to a muted gray, the first hints of light creeping over the horizon. My shift ended, and I passed the responsibility to another soldier. I exhaled deeply, feeling the tension in my shoulders begin to release, knowing I had done my part.

STORMS AND ELITE SOLDIERS

14/11/23

"5:07 PM – Today, I met soldiers from elite units, and it was inspiring. Their level of responsibility and intelligence was remarkable—every decision they made carried weight, yet they handled it with calm precision. Later, the rain began, and it brought its own challenges. The building we were stationed in, already weakened by the war, groaned under the storm. Debris fell from unstable ceilings, forcing us to stay alert even while seeking shelter. Overhead, the hum of drones continued, their presence a constant reminder of the conflict still unfolding."

MEETING THE ELITE

The day offered a rare glimpse of something extraordinary: a chance to meet soldiers from elite IDF units. These were the individuals tasked with high-stakes missions, often operating in the shadows to gather intelligence, conduct precision strikes, and handle delicate rescue operations.

Their presence was both humbling and inspiring. Despite their advanced training and enormous responsibilities, they spoke to us with camaraderie. They shared insights, practical advice, and even light-hearted stories that broke through the tension of the day. Watching them, I saw a balance of composure and focus that was nothing short of remarkable.

What struck me most was their humility. These were people who carried the weight of critical decisions, yet they didn't see themselves as superior. They reminded us of the importance of trust and teamwork, especially in moments when every second and every choice mattered.

A DANGEROUS STORM

By late afternoon, the weather shifted dramatically. The sky turned a deep gray, and heavy raindrops began to fall, quickly building into a powerful storm. The winds howled through the shattered windows and open spaces of the building, shaking its already fragile structure. The rain seeped through every crack, pooling on the floors and turning the rubble-strewn hallways into slick, hazardous paths. The storm's strength dislodged debris from above—chunks of concrete, shards of glass, and twisted metal crashed down unpredictably.

We initially tried to find the safest parts of the building, carefully watching the ceilings and keeping our gear close in case we needed to move quickly. But as the storm intensified, it became clear that staying there wasn't an option. The structure groaned under the weight of the wind, and the risks of collapse or injury grew too great.

With little choice, we grabbed our gear and evacuated the building, stepping into the relentless downpour. The rain soaked us instantly, making every step a challenge as the ground turned to slippery mud. The storm didn't just bring discomfort; it added another layer of uncertainty to an already tense situation. Outside, we regrouped under the cover of what little shelter we could find, waiting for the storm to ease. It was a stark reminder that in war, even nature could become an adversary, forcing us to adapt, stay alert, and keep moving forward.

THE DRONES

Amid the storm, the faint but persistent hum of drones continued overhead. Their presence was a reminder that even in the chaos, someone was watching over us. The military drones circling above provided critical intelligence and ensured our safety, scanning for threats we couldn't see.

But there was a duality to their sound. While friendly drones brought a sense of security, the possibility of enemy drones was ever-present. We knew Hamas was capable of deploying drones for surveillance, strikes, or even dropping explosives. The tension never fully eased, even with the reassurance of our own technology.

THE SANDWICH

15/11/23

"The storm finally passed, giving us a quieter day. We got tuna sandwiches from Aroma, a welcome treat after days of simple meals. Last night was freezing, but we took a moment to leave our mark. On the wall of the hotel, we wrote 'Nova Hotel' in memory of the Nova massacre—a small tribute to honor those we lost."

A MOMENT OF JOY

The storm had finally passed, leaving the air crisp and the skies clear, but the chill of the night still lingered in our bones. We woke up in the partially standing building that had become our temporary shelter, trying to shake off the tiredness of the previous days. Though the air was cold, there was a sense of calm that we hadn't felt in a long time.

That afternoon, something unexpected arrived. Boxes, bright and unmistakable, with the bold logo of Aroma—a beloved café chain in Israel known for its fresh coffee, sandwiches, and salads. In a place like Gaza, where every day felt like a test of endurance, seeing those boxes was like a slice of home transported to the frontlines.

In true Israeli fashion, the mood shifted instantly. The soldiers, tired and battered, couldn't help but break into dance. It was a reflex, almost—when something good happens, you celebrate. We circled around the boxes, laughing and cheering, the weight of the war momentarily lifted.

One of the soldiers, grinning from ear to ear, stepped forward to open the first box. He was careful, dragging out the moment to build suspense. We all leaned in, hoping for something—anything—that wasn't tuna. He reached inside, pulled out a sandwich, and unwrapped it as if unveiling a treasure. For a brief second, we let ourselves believe it might be chicken, maybe even schnitzel, or something entirely different.

Then, with a dramatic pause, he laughed, looked at us, and yelled, "Tuna sandwich!"

The whole unit burst into laughter. It wasn't disappointment—it was absurdity. We had been eating tuna for what felt like an eternity, and here it was again, wrapped in the comforting logo of Aroma. But this time, the tuna was dressed up, served with tomatoes, lettuce, and onions. It felt gourmet compared to the cans we had been opening for weeks.

We sat together, eating our sandwiches, laughing, and joking. It wasn't about the food anymore—it was about the moment. It reminded us of the small joys that could still exist, even here in Gaza.

HONORING THE FALLEN

Later that evening, as the sun began to set, we took some time to reflect. On the wall of the building, we decided to leave our mark. With markers and whatever we could find, we wrote

"Nova Hotel" in bold letters—a tribute to those who lost their lives in the Nova massacre. It was our way of ensuring their memory lived on, even in the heart of the chaos we were navigating.

SHIFTING PERSPECTIVES

By now, we were more than two weeks into Gaza, and something was changing within us. The hardships hadn't eased, but our perspective was shifting. We were learning how to find light in the dark, how to laugh when the world seemed to be crumbling around us, and how to celebrate even the smallest blessings. The tuna sandwiches from Aroma might not have been what we had dreamed of, but they represented something more —a reminder of home, of the life we were fighting to protect.

PART THREE
THE JOURNAL

16/11/23

"We moved to a new location, and as soon as we arrived, we began cleaning and organizing. It was an actual house of terrorists. We found RPGs, grenades, knives, uniforms, etc. We are currently surrounded by houses that Hamas has stayed in the past."

A NEW POSITION

The morning began with yet another relocation. As part of our unit's mission to clear and secure key areas, we moved to a new position deeper into Gaza. This was routine by now—arriving, organizing, and preparing the space for the days ahead.

But this time, the place we entered wasn't just any abandoned building. It was a house that had belonged to terrorists. The moment we stepped inside, the evidence of its former occupants was impossible to ignore.

UNCOVERING THE ARSENAL

The first thing we noticed was the sheer number of weapons scattered throughout the house. RPGs leaned against the walls, their presence both ominous and sobering. Grenades were tucked into corners, ready to be used at a moment's notice. Knives and uniforms, stained and tattered, spoke to the lives that had once operated here.

Every item we found told a story. This wasn't just a house—it was a base, a hub for planning and executing violence.

The sight of the weapons was a harsh reminder of the stakes of our mission. These weren't abstract threats; they were tangible, deadly tools that could have been used against us or against innocent civilians.

CLEARING THE SPACE

Our first task was to clear and secure the house, making it safe for us to use. We moved carefully, checking every room, every drawer, every shadow for hidden dangers. The process was meticulous, a mix of adrenaline and focus.

The house wasn't an isolated instance. As we settled in, we realized we were surrounded by similar homes, all of which had been occupied by Hamas at some point. The area was a maze of past operations, a reminder of how deeply entrenched the enemy was in this city.

Every step outside the house felt heavy, the weight of the location pressing down on all of us. The knowledge that these streets had been the backdrop for so much suffering was hard to shake.

FIRST ONES IN, LAST ONES OUT

17/11/23

"The news hit yesterday: another 30 days in Gaza, 'first ones in, last ones out.' It was tough to process, especially as we'd been holding onto hope this would end soon. The mental battle feels heavier now. Last night, one of the soldiers had his first PTSD attack, jumping at every sound. I sat with him, offering quiet support. Sometimes, just being there is enough. Today was better. We finally got to shower and change uniforms, pure relief after weeks in the same gear. Before long, we spotted two Hamas missiles streaking toward Israel. Watching them disappear into the distance filled us with a mix of tension and relief, a stark reminder of why we were here. Later, I joined one of the tanks that was taking soldiers with the heaviest equipment back to our location. The ride was chaotic, every movement unpredictable, but the crew's calmness inspired me."

THE WEIGHT OF THIRTY MORE DAYS

The announcement came like a punch to the gut. Thirty more days in Gaza. When the major shared the news, the energy in the room shifted instantly. Until now, most of us had clung to the hope that we'd be out within a week, back home with our families, walking out of Gaza with the Israeli flag held high.

But "first ones in and last ones out" wasn't just a phrase; it was a reality. We were here to finish the mission, no matter how long it took. The realization was heavy, and it became clear that the greatest battle wasn't with the enemy—it was with ourselves. Mentally, the toll of this war was growing heavier by the day.

PTSD STRUGGLE

That night, Yoram had his first PTSD attack. It began with a sudden jump every time he heard an explosion or a gunshot, his body reacting instinctively to the sounds around us. By the time the night deepened, he couldn't sleep at all.

I sat beside him, unsure of what to say but knowing I had to say something. In a quiet voice, I told him, "Hey, I have no idea what PTSD feels like, although what I do know is that it feels good to have someone to talk to when you're going through these hard times. I'm here for you if you need anything."

It wasn't much, but it was honest. He nodded, his eyes reflecting the struggle inside him. I couldn't take away his pain, but I sat beside him for the rest of the night and hoped my words reminded him that he wasn't alone.

THE MISSILES

Two Hamas missiles streaked across the horizon, cutting through the air with terrifying precision. We stood there in silence, watching them tear through the sky, and my heart sank. Knowing they were aimed at Israel—at the very people I was here to protect—was almost too much to bear. My mind raced to my family, my friends, and the countless innocent lives below, unaware of the danger hurtling toward them.

Anger built inside me, a deep, simmering rage at the senselessness of it all. But before that anger could consume me, I saw it—the Iron Dome. Its precision was breathtaking, its purpose clear. The interceptors shot up and met the missiles in midair, reducing them to harmless debris before they could reach their targets.

The relief was palpable, a wave of gratitude washing over me. For a moment, the anger ebbed, replaced by a renewed sense of purpose. This was why we were here—to stop those missiles, to protect what mattered most.

THE REENERGIZING DAY

The next morning, we were given a rare gift: a re-energizing day. For the first time in three weeks, we had the chance to shower and change our uniforms.

The feeling of freezing cold water on my skin was indescribable. Weeks of sweat, dirt, and sand washed away, leaving me feeling like a new person. Changing into fresh clothes was equally transformative, a small act that carried an immense sense of relief. Later, I sat with my friend as the day wound down. We watched the sunset together, its warm colors painting the sky in stark contrast to the harsh reality we were living in.

THE TANK EXPERIENCE

As the day came to a close, our commander chose three of us to return to our location in the tanks. I was selected because of the heavy equipment I carried, and while I didn't know what to expect, I was eager for the experience.

Climbing into the tank was like stepping into a different world. Inside, the space was tight and chaotic, every movement unpredictable. From the outside, tanks seemed invincible, but inside, it became clear how much precision and teamwork it took to operate them.

The tank soldiers were a different breed—calm, focused, and full of camaraderie. As we rumbled through the terrain, they shared stories and even sang a song, one that had been passed down through years of war—a reminder of everything they had endured and survived.

THE LIGHT AT THE END OF THE TUNNEL

18/11/23

"Last night, we slept in the hallway of an abandoned school—a cold, uncomfortable refuge. At one point, we gathered without the commanders to share what we were going through. I gave a short speech: 'This isn't just a physical battle; it's mental. Focus on the light at the end of the tunnel.' For a moment, we felt united, ready to press on. Later, snipers spotted ten terrorists running to a nearby building. We alerted a nearby unit, and they quickly took action. At dawn, we relocated, searching houses and uncovering weapons, masks, flags, and uniforms—stark reminders of the enemy's presence. Every moment of the mission tested our focus and determination, but quitting was never an option."

THE HALLWAY REFUGE

The night in the abandoned school was another test of endurance. Our makeshift shelter was a cold, narrow hallway with cracked walls that let in the biting night air. The broken windows revealed fragments of the shattered world outside, a stark reminder of where we were. Sleep was elusive, the hard floor pressing against our backs and the constant tension keeping us on edge.

A MEETING OF MINDS

With exhaustion creeping in, we took a rare moment to sit together without the commanders. It wasn't a formal meeting, but more of an unspoken agreement to share what was weighing on us. For weeks, our conversations had circled the same frustrations, a loop of fear and uncertainty with no way forward.

I stood up, sensing the need to say something that could cut through the heaviness. "Three weeks have passed," I began. "We've been having the same conversations, stuck in the same mindset. This isn't just about our bodies anymore—it's about our minds."

The group was quiet, listening intently as I continued. "We're all fighting battles, not just out there," I gestured toward the broken windows, "but in here," I said, tapping my head.

I shared a quote that had stayed with me: "If you change the way you look at things, the things you look at will change."

I continued, my voice steady, "We need to stop thinking about how much longer we'll be here. Instead, let's focus on the light at the end of the tunnel. It's there. We just have to keep moving toward it."

The room fell silent, the words sinking in. For a brief moment, it felt like we weren't just surviving—we were finding a purpose in pushing forward.

THE MISSION

The calm was short-lived. Snipers alerted us to movement: ten terrorists were seen running into a nearby building. The announcement shattered our brief respite, and we quickly alerted a nearby unit, trusting them to handle the situation.

Later, we relocated to a new area and began our search inside the buildings. The air was thick with tension as we moved through each house, rifles raised, scanning every corner.

One house held uniforms and masks neatly stored away, ready for use. Another displayed Hamas flags hanging on the walls, their defiance a sharp contrast to the silence of the deserted streets. We confiscated weapons and gear, small victories in a larger fight. Each find was a reminder of the enemy's presence, a chilling testament to their preparation and intent.

THE BATTLE WITHIN

As the day went on, my thoughts returned to the earlier meeting. The battle wasn't just with the terrorists hiding in the shadows—it was with ourselves. The relentless pace and the gnawing uncertainty tested every ounce of our strength.

But we moved forward, one mission at a time, one house at a time. Each step was a reminder that we were inching closer to the light at the end of the tunnel. It wasn't easy, but it was necessary. Together, we pressed on, determined to find that light, no matter how far it seemed.

FIRE AND RAIN

19/11/23

"This morning, I woke up to Ofir's voice as he talked about the AK-47 he had found. We went back to the room where it was discovered and uncovered more Hamas flags and masks. The AK-47 and other items were handed over to a special unit for further analysis. Later in the day, during a mission, I fired 250 bullets toward a building we had to clear. On the way back, heavy rain soaked us, making every step through the mud a challenge. Now, at 19:34, I'm finally lying down, ready for whatever tomorrow brings."

HIDDEN THREATS

The morning began with Ofir's familiar voice pulling me from sleep. His excitement cut through the grogginess as he talked about the AK-47 we had found the day before. There was something surreal about waking up to a discussion of weapons like it was any other topic, but such was life here.

We went back to the room where it was discovered, this time combing through every corner more thoroughly. It was a strange, unsettling experience. Among the debris of what was once a home, we found more than just weapons. Hamas flags and masks were stashed away in the parents' bedroom, but the chilling discovery came in the children's room. On the top shelves, hidden among toys and books, were more weapons and materials.

It was a gut-wrenching moment—proof of how deeply this conflict ran, how it reached even into spaces that were once filled with laughter and innocence. In that room, we saw two worlds collide: a child's forgotten toys lying beside a hidden cache of weapons. There were faded storybooks, soft stuffed animals with missing eyes, and a school notebook still open on the floor. But behind a loose panel in the wall, there were rifles, loaded magazines, and a folded flag.

It didn't feel real. For a second, I imagined a child sitting there not long ago, drawing pictures or practicing reading aloud—completely unaware of what was being hidden behind the same walls. It was more than disturbing; it was devastating. That room had been a place of safety, of learning, and imagination. But now it was nothing more than another battlefield.

The contrast hit all of us hard. One of my teammates stood silently, staring at a pair of tiny shoes left neatly by the doorway, just inches from a grenade we had found tucked beneath the bed. No words were needed. We all felt it.

That moment exposed a brutal truth: generations were growing up with war baked into the walls of their homes. In places where there should've been bedtime stories, there were battle plans. It reminded me exactly why we were there. We weren't just fighting to push back terror—we were fighting for the right of children to grow up without ever having to know what a gun sounds like. For homes to stay homes, and not become armories. For the chance to break the cycle that turns bedrooms into battlegrounds. The AK-47 and other items were handed over to a special unit for further analysis. These finds weren't just weapons—they were pieces of the puzzle in this war, tools that could help us understand and dismantle the enemy's network.

THE MISSION

Later in the day, we set out on a mission that required clearing a building suspected of harboring threats. My role was clear: to provide cover fire when necessary. I fired 250 bullets that day, each one deliberate, each one necessary. The crack of the machine gun was deafening, the recoil familiar but still demanding.

The adrenaline coursed through me as we completed the mission, the building now secured. There was no time to dwell on what we'd done or what we'd found. Slowly and steadily, the pitter-patter of the raindrops turned the dusty streets into a treacherous, muddy mess.

THE RAIN AND THE RETURN

The rain wasn't just an inconvenience—it was a new challenge. The ground became slick, every step a careful calculation to avoid slipping while staying alert to any possible threats. Moving quickly was nearly impossible. Each step required balance and focus, the mud pulling at our boots as if it wanted to hold us back.

The weight of our gear felt heavier than ever, soaked through with rainwater. But we couldn't let our guard down. Even in the rain, the danger was ever-present. Every shadow, every sound, was a potential threat, and we had to stay sharp.

By the time we reached our location, we were drenched. The rain had soaked through our uniforms, chilling us to the bone. But there was also a strange sense of relief—another mission completed, another step closer to safety.

ROCKET LAUNCHER

20/11/23

"We set out at 5:00 AM with orders to destroy a rocket launcher hidden in a school. Before entering, we carefully cleared the area to avoid any ambushes. By evening, I was assigned to guard the dark entrance of our building. The wind made every sound sharper, keeping me on edge with my finger on the trigger. Waking the next group for their guarding shift was tough. Despite the fatigue, we pushed through and completed the mission."

THE MISSION

The day began early, our orders clear: reach an elementary school where Hamas had hidden a rocket launcher, clear the area, and destroy the threat. At 5:00 AM, we moved with precision and heightened awareness, knowing Hamas often used places like schools, which seemed vulnerable, to hide weapons and launch attacks. Their strategy of using these locations wasn't just tactical; it was psychological, a way to make their operations harder to combat without creating collateral damage.

Clearing the area was tense. Every corner, every shadow, could conceal a threat. As we approached the school, I couldn't ignore the weight of knowing what the launcher represented. From where I stood, missiles had been fired toward Israel—toward my brothers and sisters, toward the people I loved. That thought fueled every step, every breath.

When we reached the launcher, it was hard to take in. The weapon, stark and menacing, stood as a grim reminder of the stakes. We secured it and prepared for its destruction, knowing each action brought us closer to safety for those back home.

INSIDE THE SCHOOL

Entering the school, we conducted a thorough search of the building. What we found was sobering. Among the books and materials scattered throughout the classrooms were propaganda tools aimed at the youngest generation. The curriculum was filled with hatred, indoctrinating children to despise Jewish people from an early age. Seeing it firsthand was heartbreaking—a systematic effort to turn innocence into hostility. It was difficult to process, knowing that such hatred was planted in minds so young.

GUARD DUTY IN THE DARK

Later that evening, I was assigned to guard the entrance of our building. The cold crept in as darkness enveloped everything. I lay on the ground, my machine gun steady and my senses sharp. The wind made the structure groan, each creak of metal sending my pulse racing. Animals moved through the rubble, their steps indistinguishable from potential threats at times. Every sound—no matter how small—forced me to remain on edge, my finger ready on the trigger.

The silence wasn't peaceful; it was heavy with the possibility of danger. Hours stretched on, and fatigue tried to claw at my focus, but I stayed vigilant, knowing that any lapse could mean a disaster.

WAKING THE NEXT SHIFT

At around 4:00 AM, it was time to wake the next group for their shift. This task was nearly as challenging as staying alert during my watch. Exhaustion had taken its toll on everyone. Some soldiers wouldn't stir even after a hard slap across the face. Their bodies had reached a point of pure fatigue.

I did my best to motivate them with my words, pulling them up and encouraging them to take their positions as quickly as possible. It wasn't just about orders—it was about trust. Each of us relied on the other to ensure our safety, and I couldn't let them falter, no matter how drained we all felt.

CONVERSATIONS AND SEARCHES

21/11/23

"This morning started with a simple breakfast: a tuna sandwich and a protein bar. I spent some time talking with the tank soldiers, learning about the meaning behind their songs. It was interesting to hear the stories and traditions they carry with them. Later, my friends and I continued searching for illegal weapons, staying focused on the mission ahead."

A SIMPLE START

The morning began with quiet simplicity, a brief moment of calm in the midst of chaos. As the sun rose over the scarred landscape of Gaza, I sat on a chunk of broken concrete that had once been part of a wall. My breakfast—a tuna sandwich and a protein bar—was far from memorable, but it was enough to fuel the day ahead. In a place like this, even the smallest routines felt grounding.

CONVERSATIONS WITH THE TANK CREW

After eating, I joined some of the tank soldiers nearby. These men had a calm, steady presence, shaped by their experience and the sheer responsibility of operating such massive machines. Their stories intrigued me, from navigating the cramped interior of a tank during missions to the precision required in urban combat.

One of them explained the songs they sing during missions, each one carrying a story of resilience and solidarity. Listening to them talk about their tanks as if they were old friends—machines with quirks and personalities—was unexpectedly comforting. It was a reminder of the connection and trust we all relied on, whether with our gear or with each other.

SEARCHING FOR WEAPONS

The rest of the morning was spent on a task we'd become all too familiar with: searching for illegal weapons. Alongside my closest friends in the unit, we combed through houses reduced to rubble, checking every nook and cranny. The work demanded focus. Every drawer, hollow space, or loose floor tile could hide something dangerous. Each find was a reminder of the constant danger around us, but also a small victory. With every weapon confiscated, we chipped away at the enemy's ability to harm others, inching closer to the sense of security we all longed for.

WHISPERS OF HOPE

22/11/23

"This morning, as we ate, rumors of a ceasefire and hostages being released spread among us. Smiles broke through the exhaustion, and for a moment, hope filled the air. We've been in the same spot for days, but this news feels like a light at the end of the tunnel."

A GLIMMER OF HOPE

The day began like any other, with us gathering around to eat a simple breakfast. The air was heavy with the usual tension that had become part of our daily existence. But then, whispers began to ripple through the group—rumors of a ceasefire.

At first, we were hesitant to believe it. A ceasefire? After everything we'd been through? But as the whispers grew louder and the possibility became more real, a wave of cautious optimism spread through us.

When someone finally confirmed the news, the reaction was immediate. Smiles cracked tired faces, and for the first time in days, I saw something that resembled joy. It wasn't just the possibility of a break in the fighting that lifted our spirits—it was the hope that hostages might finally be released and brought back to Israel.

The idea of those families reuniting after weeks of unimaginable fear and pain was enough to make us forget, if only briefly, about the rubble surrounding us. It was a moment that reminded us why we were here.

For days, we had been stationed in the same location, surrounded by destruction, trying to stay focused and alert. But that morning, for the first time in a long while, the thought of going home didn't feel like just a distant dream. It felt like a possibility—something worth holding onto.

Hope doesn't end wars, but it gives you the strength to keep fighting until they do. And on that morning, hope was enough.

THE CLEARING MISSION

23/11/23

"At 04:25, I woke a few soldiers for a mission with the elite explosives unit. By 05:00, we joined other units and tanks under a building to clear a strip of road from terrorists, mines, and tunnels. I carried 300 bullets, the weight making every step harder as we ran across debris-filled terrain. At one point, I almost slipped, but I managed to keep going. When my commander gave the order to fire, I dropped to one knee and unleashed 120 bullets in one burst."

THE ROAD TO CLEAR

The morning of November 23 began before the first light. At 04:25, I was tasked with waking a few soldiers for an important mission. It was no easy feat—everyone was running on fumes from the relentless cycle of missions and guard duty. Sleep had become a luxury we could no longer afford, and the effects were starting to show.

No matter how strong a person is, the human body isn't built to function properly without sleep. The lack of rest slows you down, clouds your judgment, and makes every task feel heavier. But in war, there's no pause button.

By 05:00, we were ready. We met with an elite team specializing in explosives and tunnel warfare, along with a convoy of tanks beneath a heavily damaged building. The mission was straightforward but critical: clear a new strip of road from potential threats—terrorists, mines, and tunnels.

A RACE AGAINST THE CLOCK

As soon as the mission began, it was all about speed. Every step, every decision, had to be swift and precise. We moved quickly, running across uneven terrain littered with debris. The weight of my gear—a machine gun, 300 bullets, and my vest—pressed down on me with every step.

The fatigue made every movement feel exaggerated, as if I were running through molasses. At one point, I felt my foot slip on a jagged piece of concrete. My balance wavered, but my other foot caught me just in time to avoid hitting the ground. The scare jolted me awake, and I pressed forward to keep pace with my unit.

The road ahead wasn't forgiving—twisted metal, loose rocks, and remnants of buildings made it a gauntlet. We moved in a tight formation, knowing full well that any misstep could expose us to unseen dangers.

120 BULLETS

As we neared a suspected hotspot, my commander's voice cut through the morning stillness: "Fire now!" Instinct took over. I dropped to one knee, my machine gun steady in my hands, and let loose 120 bullets in one continuous burst. The sound was deafening, echoing through the ruined streets like a thunderclap.

When I looked up, I saw the astonished faces of my friends. Their expressions said it all—shock mixed with respect. In moments like this, it's about instinct, training, and doing what needs to be done.

A TEST OF RESTRAINT

24/11/23

"At 04:30, we scrambled to wake tired soldiers for a mission. Once ready, we secured a house suspected of hiding weapons and tunnels while a unit set explosives. A massive fireball soon lit the sky, marking progress. I was then ordered to the fifth floor of a nearby building and fired 200 rounds at a suspicious target where a terrorist was spotted. Later, during my guarding shift, we received confirmation of a ceasefire deal with strict rules to hold fire unless directly threatened. Mid-shift, we spotted six terrorists running into a building 350 meters away. My finger was on the trigger, but the order to hold fire kept me steady. The release of hostages made restraint the only choice. It was a tense balance of action and patience."

THE CEASEFIRE

The morning began with tension running high. At 04:30, we struggled to rouse our soldiers for a critical mission. Once gathered, we moved swiftly to a location suspected of harboring weapons and tunnels. Our job was to secure the area while another unit planted explosives. As we held our positions, the explosive team completed their task, and moments later, the sky lit up with a massive fireball. The mission wasn't over.

I was ordered back to a nearby building and up to the fifth floor. The climb was quick, my boots pounding the stairs, my body on autopilot. Reaching the top, I was immediately directed to fire at a suspicious target—a terrorist seen setting something up. Dropping to a knee, I unleashed 200 rounds, each shot echoing in the tense silence of the early morning.

THE CEASEFIRE CONFIRMATION

After the mission, breakfast with my friends was a rare moment of reprieve. But it was short-lived. During our meal, we received the long-awaited confirmation: the ceasefire deal was officially in place. Hostages would begin their return to Israel, and our orders were clear—follow the ceasefire rules to the letter. It felt like a small victory. But the reality of what those rules entailed hit hard later that day during my guarding shift.

SIX TERRORISTS

As the afternoon stillness enveloped us, a sudden movement caught our eyes—six terrorists, one by one, emerging from a hole in the ground. They moved quickly, sprinting toward a nearby building just 350 meters from our location.

Every instinct in my body screamed to shoot. My finger hovered over the trigger, ready to act. The image of them disappearing into another building churned in my gut. My brain wrestled with the raw danger they represented—terrorists on the move, likely planning their next attack—against the image of innocent children being reunited with their families.

This was one of the hardest decisions I've ever had to make. I knew I could hit them. My training had prepared me for this moment, and the proximity all but guaranteed a successful shot. But the hostage deal stood above everything else. Breaking the ceasefire would put those children, our hostages, at risk.

At that moment, I understood the depth of our mission. From the second I stepped into Gaza, this was why we fought—not for revenge, but for the lives of those who had been stolen from us.

FAITH IN THE DARKNESS

25/11/23

"Haven't slept in so long, and I feel sick with no energy, although I have a warm feeling in my heart because I was notified that 13 children were released from captivity and returned to Israel last night. Knowing that I took part in saving these innocent children is very special to me. In four days, I will be completing a month in Gaza. Feels like it's an endless process, although, like I said, there is one thing that I have that keeps me moving forward. It's faith—emunah."

A HEAVY HEART

The physical toll of Gaza was catching up to me. Each day drained my energy more than the last. Every unit had a combat medic with us at all times, carrying a heavy bag full of essential medical gear. If a soldier wasn't feeling well, they'd assess the situation on the spot. In more serious cases—especially if the mission allowed—it was possible to be evacuated out of Gaza, though depending on the conditions, that could take hours or even days. But most of us, unless it was urgent, just pushed through. That's what the job demanded.

THE CHILDREN'S RETURN

The news spread through our unit like a quiet ripple: Hamas had released 24 hostages—including 13 Israelis, along with 10 Thai nationals and 1 Filipino. It was the first day of the ceasefire, November 24. Among the Israelis were women and children, including four young kids, just 2, 4, 6, and 9 years old. I remember hearing those ages and going still. You couldn't help but picture them—tiny, innocent, probably terrified, and now finally… free.

For weeks, we had been locked in a cycle of movement, alertness, adrenaline, and survival. You lose track of time in Gaza. You lose track of everything but the mission. And then something like this happens, and it knocks the wind out of you—not in a bad way, but in a *human* way.

I had to sit down. It was hard to process.

Because this—this was what it was all for.

Thirteen people taken from their homes were now back in Israel. Back with their families. These weren't numbers. These were daughters, sons, sisters, mothers. Children who had spent 49 days in captivity, in fear, are now breathing air on their side of the border. Alive. Safe.

I thought about what it must have felt like for their parents. I imagined the moment of reunion—arms wrapped tight, tears streaming, not believing they were real, still whole, still theirs.

And then I thought about my role—small, maybe, but still part of the larger effort that helped make that moment possible. Whether it was holding a position, running missions to clear neighborhoods, or simply showing up every day ready to follow orders, I had been part of this mission from the start. Our unit had worked nonstop to keep the pressure on, to secure the areas we were assigned, and to help build the conditions that led to this ceasefire.

I couldn't stop thinking about the children. How do you explain war to a 2-year-old? Or a 6-year-old who's just learned to read? What nightmares will they carry for the rest of their lives?

And then I looked around at my team. We were dirty, bruised, some of us limping from old injuries. But there was light in our eyes again—real, visible light. Because no matter how much pain we'd gone through, *this* was a moment of purpose. This was hope.

REFLECTION AMID THE STRUGGLE

As I wrote in my notebook, I couldn't help but think about the children's journey ahead. The trauma they had endured wouldn't disappear overnight, but I believed in their resilience. Children have a remarkable way of healing, of finding joy even in the darkest moments.

It struck me how this war wasn't just about fighting enemies or securing land—it was about protecting futures. Every mission we completed, every sacrifice we made, was for moments like this: the safe return of the innocent.

A MONTH IN GAZA

The days in Gaza had begun to blur together, the missions, the sounds, the smells all melding into a relentless cycle. In just four days, I would reach a month since crossing the border—a milestone that felt both significant and surreal.

Time in Gaza moved differently. Each hour stretched endlessly, yet the weeks slipped by in a haze of adrenaline. It was easy to lose perspective, to feel like the process would never end.

But there was something that kept me grounded: my faith—*emunah.*

THE POWER OF EMUNAH

Faith had been my anchor throughout this war. It was the belief that, despite the chaos, there was a purpose to everything we endured. It was the hope that our actions, no matter how small, were part of a greater plan.

In the darkest moments, when my body felt like giving out and my mind spiraled into doubt, *emunah* pulled me back. It reminded me that this wasn't forever, that there was a light at the end of the tunnel.

A SONG IN THE SILENCE

26/11/23

"At 11:40 AM, I left to fix my machine gun, which had a trigger issue. We walked 1.5 kilometers at a fast pace and barely made it to a meeting with our magad, the lead captain. He shared sad news about the deaths of soldiers fighting in other sections and informed us we'd be heading out for a few days due to the ceasefire. Back at the building, we discovered a working radio. It was a rare moment of relief—everyone gathered around, singing together and lifting each other's spirits."

THE RADIO

The day started with urgency. At 11:40 AM, I set out to fix my machine gun, which had developed a problem with the trigger. It wasn't a task I could afford to put off, not in a place like this. After the repair, we set off on a fast-paced walk, covering 1.5 kilometers to meet with our *magad*, the lead captain.

We arrived just in time, sweat dripping down our faces, to hear the news. The magad stood before us, his voice steady but heavy with grief. He informed us about soldiers who had fallen in other sections of Gaza, a stark reminder of the cost of this war. The air felt thick with emotion, but he also told us something lighter: because of the ceasefire, we'd be leaving Gaza for a few days.

The news sparked a glimmer of hope. For weeks, we'd been living in a state of constant tension, and the idea of stepping back, even briefly, felt like a weight being lifted.

A RARE FIND

Back at our location, we stumbled across something unexpected —a small, battered radio tucked away in the corner of a room. It didn't look like much, but when we turned it on, the faint sound of music came through.

The soldiers gathered around it like moths to a flame. The music was hard to make out at first, crackling and distorted, but the familiar tunes slowly emerged. One by one, smiles appeared on our faces.

It was such a simple thing, yet it carried immense power. We sang together, our voices blending with the static, filling the broken walls of the building with a rare sense of joy. For a moment, the war felt distant.

A SHARED MOMENT

I watched the faces of my friends as they sang. There was something pure about the moment—no one thinking about the next mission, the dangers outside, or the weight of the news we had just received. For a few minutes, we were just young men, connected by a shared love for the music that reminded us of home.

CHAPTER 11
THE ROAD BACK TO ISRAEL

27/11/23

"The day started with guardian duty, where Avi taught me a few Arabic words—small lessons to pass the time. Our exit from Gaza was delayed from 10:00 to 15:00 due to rain and waiting for another unit to take our place. When the hammers finally arrived, we moved quickly and silently in the darkness, their lights off to avoid detection. I sat in the last vehicle, my machine gun ready, scanning the surroundings as we sped along the same path we'd entered weeks before. The wind rushed past my helmet, bringing a flood of memories—our missions, the challenges, and the bonds we'd formed."

LEAVING GAZA

The morning began like any other—guardian duty, eyes scanning the horizon, ears tuned to every sound in the stillness of the morning. My friend Avi stood beside me, and during a lull, he began teaching me a few words in Arabic. It was a small but meaningful distraction. Learning even a little bit of the language felt like bridging an unseen divide, a way of understanding the world around me better, even amidst the chaos.

Our unit was scheduled to leave Gaza at 10:00 hours, a moment we had been waiting for with equal parts anticipation and exhaustion. But the rain had other plans. An unusually heavy downpour turned the rubble-strewn ground into mud, and our departure was delayed to 15:00 hours. We waited, huddled together, while new soldiers arrived to take our positions.

When the time finally came, the sun had set, plunging everything into darkness. The hammers arrived silently, their engines humming faintly against the steady rhythm of rain. We moved quickly but cautiously, keeping noise and light to a minimum. Every step out of that building felt like shedding the weight of weeks of stress.

THE RIDE OUT

I was assigned to the last hammer in the line, my machine gun stationed and ready, placed on top of the hammer's wheel. As we sped through the darkened path, retracing the route we had entered, the cool night air rushed past my helmet. It carried with it a strange mix of emotions—relief and a quiet sadness I couldn't fully explain.

Somewhere in the hum of the engine and the weight of silence, I reached into my vest and pulled out the journal I had carried with me from day one. Somehow, it was still there—tucked safely in the top pocket where I had kept it through every mission, every sprint, every moment I thought I might not make it back. I reached into another pocket and found the pen I had been using. It wasn't crushed or lost, and somehow, it still had ink.

That small discovery meant more than I could explain. It was like a reminder that both the journal and I had made it back in one piece.

I didn't write anything, though—the hammer jolted sharply with every bump in the road, and my eyes had to stay alert. My focus remained locked in, my hands still ready. It wasn't the time to write—not yet.

My thoughts swirled as I looked out into the night. This was the same path we had entered weeks ago, under the cover of darkness, our nerves on edge, every shadow a potential threat. Now, it felt different. We had left our mark on this place, putting in hard, relentless work to complete every mission. I felt proud, but there was also a sense of finality in my chest.

My upper back throbbed with sharp pain, a lingering injury from days of carrying heavy gear and firing my machine gun. As the hammer bounced over the uneven terrain, I realized that this pain might mean I wouldn't be coming back to Gaza with my unit. That thought sat heavy in my mind, an unspoken farewell to the place that had tested us in ways I could never have imagined.

BACK IN ISRAEL

When we crossed back into Israel, the tension lifted almost immediately. There was no cheering—just quiet relief. I looked at my friends and saw the same expression on every face. We didn't need to say anything. We all knew what we had been through.

At the base, we were handed warm clothes and blankets. The cold felt sharper now, maybe because everything was finally sinking in.

I pulled out my journal and the same pen I'd carried the entire time. Somehow, it had made it through with me—uncrushed, still working. I wrote down how it felt to be back. The weight. The relief. The stillness after so much chaos.

And when I finished that last line, I paused.

I knew right then that this was it—the final entry. The journal that had carried every emotion, every fear, every small moment of strength ... was now full. I closed it gently, knowing that with it, I had also closed one of the hardest, most defining chapters of my life.

CHAPTER 12
UNMASKING THE PRESENT

A CALL TO HOME

Coming back to Israel after 30 days in Gaza felt like stepping into another world. Thirty days—it doesn't sound like much, but it felt like an eternity. When we first crossed the border into Gaza, we thought we'd be there for a week, maybe two at most. That's what I had told my parents when I reassured them over the phone. "Everything will be fine," I had said. "I'll be back before you know it." But days turned into weeks, and weeks into a full month.

The anticipation of leaving Gaza had built slowly, an almost surreal hope that began to creep into our minds as the missions wound down and whispers of a ceasefire began to circulate. Yet, when we finally crossed back into Israel, it didn't feel real. It was hard to believe that the place that had tested us, pushed us, and forced us to confront our limits was behind us now

A WARM WELCOME

When we arrived back at the base, we were met with an overwhelming wave of kindness. Families from across Israel had sent food, warm clothes, and blankets for us. Tables overflowed with home-cooked meals—lasagnas, schnitzels, fresh bread, and steaming pots of soup. The aroma filled the air, wrapping us in the kind of warmth that reminded us of home.

I stood there, taking it all in, and felt a deep sense of gratitude. These weren't just donations—they were acts of love, reminders that people had been thinking about us, praying for us, and doing whatever they could to make us feel appreciated.

For the first time in weeks, I let myself exhale. I let myself feel the comfort of being surrounded by my brothers, wrapped in the care of strangers who felt like family. It wasn't just physical comfort; it was the emotional weight that was lifted when we saw how much people cared. Some of the soldiers who had known me before Gaza stared for a moment before smiling. One friend said quietly, "You've changed, achi ... you look older." Another clapped my shoulder and added, "Not in a bad way—you just have that mature look in your eyes now." It was the first time I realized they could see something in me I couldn't yet name. A few hours later, we were told something that brought another wave of anticipation—the families of our entire unit had been informed that we were coming back to Israel, and they had been given permission to come visit us. We were also told that we'd be heading to a park to meet them all in person.

I didn't know who, if anyone, would be there for me. None of my biological family was in Israel, but deep down, I had a feeling my adoptive family might come.

When we finally arrived at the park, the buses pulled up one by one. Through the window, I watched the scene unfold—sons and daughters stepping off, instantly swallowed into the arms of their families. Parents held onto their children like they would never let go, tears streaming down their faces. It was a miracle we were all back in one piece. The air was thick with emotion—happy tears, laughter, and relief.

When my turn came, I stepped off the bus with the MAG machine gun still slung over my shoulder. I could feel the stares —some families cheered, others just looked at me in silence, their eyes telling stories words never could. And then I saw her—

Yam, my former Hebrew teacher, who had become family to me through my adoptive family.

I dropped the gun and wrapped her in a hug. Seeing her there filled me with a joy I didn't even realize I'd been holding back. She pulled back slightly, looked me over, and laughed, "Wow ... what a beard. And your hair!" She wasn't wrong—I had heavy bags under my eyes from the exhaustion, and my beard and hair had grown wild.

She bent down, trying to lift the machine gun, and asked how I managed to carry it all this time. I told her, "It was all to protect your family and mine. We, as Jewish people, are all brothers and sisters—that's my motivation."

As we walked together, other soldiers waved me over, inviting me to eat with their families—including one of my commanders, who knew I was a lone soldier. In that moment, surrounded by warmth and acceptance, I felt like I truly belonged.

HUNDREDS OF MESSAGES

After we settled in, we were finally given our phones back. Mine had been buried deep in my bag, untouched for weeks. When I pressed the power button, nothing happened. It had been dead for so long that it needed an hour to charge before it turned on.

The moment it came to life, the screen exploded with notifications. Hundreds of messages appeared one after another, from friends, family, and even distant acquaintances. Everyone was checking up on me, wanting to know if I was okay, if I was still alive.

It was overwhelming. I didn't know where to start. How could I possibly answer them all at once? I sent quick replies to reassure them: "I'm okay. I made it out." But with every message I read, I felt the weight of how many people had been worrying about me every single day I was in Gaza.

THE PHONE CALL

Later that night, when the adrenaline of being back began to fade, I wandered outside to find a spot with good phone reception. I needed to call my parents. The first few attempts were frustrating—my mom's voice was faint, distorted by the weak signal. "Hello? Are you there?" she asked, her worry evident even through the crackling line.

After several tries, I found a spot where the signal held. Finally, I heard her clearly. "I can hear you now!" she said, and the relief in her voice was enough to bring tears to my eyes.

We talked for what felt like hours. She asked about everything—my health, my friends, whether I was eating enough. Her questions were simple, but they were exactly what I needed. For the first time in weeks, I felt like her son again, not just a soldier.

Then she handed the phone to my dad.

From the first word he spoke, I could tell something was different. His voice trembled, filled with emotion he was struggling to contain. And for the first time in my life, I realized my father was crying.

He wasn't crying out of weakness—far from it. He was crying because he had been strong for too long. He told me about the nights he had spent sitting at home with my mom, waiting for updates and praying not to hear my name among the fallen. My siblings, who lived in different parts of the country, had all booked flights home as soon as they heard I was going to war. For the first time in years, the entire family was together again, united by the fear of losing me. He also said something I didn't expect: "When you speak now ... you speak slower. Like every word matters." I didn't notice it until he said it, but maybe Gaza had taught me to measure my words the way I had learned to measure every step inside those streets.

As my dad explained all of this, a thought struck me that I couldn't shake: why does it take something as devastating as war to bring people together? Why do we wait until someone gets married or passes away to see our loved ones?

I wished, more than anything, that we as human beings could take the time to cherish those around us. To hug our parents more, to ask our siblings how their day was, to share even the smallest moments together before it's too late.

A HEAVY REFLECTION

That night, after the call, I sat alone with my thoughts. The pain of what my parents had endured—the endless waiting, the constant fear—stayed with me. I thought about my dad's tears, the strength it took for him to hold everything together for so long, and the sacrifice my family had made just by letting me go.

It wasn't just my family. It was every family in Israel—every parent, every sibling, every child waiting and praying for their loved ones to return. This war tested us in ways we never imagined, but it also revealed the power of unity, love, and the unbreakable spirit that binds us together.

As I lay down that night, I promised myself that I would never take my family for granted. And I promised that when I returned home, I would hug my parents a little tighter, ask my siblings about their day, and remind them just how much they mean to me.

CHAPTER 13
FROM THE FRONT LINES TO A NEW FIGHT

The morning after we returned from Gaza, I was taken to a specialist to evaluate the pain in my back. For weeks, I had carried the FN MAG machine gun—loaded, heavy, and constantly ready—as we moved across broken terrain under pressure and fire. That weapon became more than just a tool. It was a symbol of trust, responsibility, and strength. I carried it with pride, even as my body began to break down under its weight.

The doctor examined me, ran several posture and spinal alignment tests, and then sat quietly for a moment before speaking. His tone was serious.

"You're developing kyphosis," he said. "It's already affecting your posture, and if you keep operating the MAG, it will almost certainly worsen. Possibly permanently."

Kyphosis. I had heard the word before, but I didn't fully understand what it meant until that moment. It wasn't just back pain—it was a progressive spinal curvature. My back had begun to round and arch unnaturally. My shoulders pulled forward. My posture, once upright and ready, had started collapsing inward without me realizing it.

The doctor leaned forward and spoke plainly. "You can't keep carrying that weapon. Not if you want to avoid long-term damage. You need to stop—immediately."

He signed a paper granting me permission to rest and recover. I was being pulled from the front lines—not because I had failed, but because my body had reached its limit. I wasn't being dismissed—I was being reassigned to a different task. One that would still serve, still protect, just in a different way. I didn't argue. I didn't fight it. But I also didn't feel relief.

A soldier who had fought alongside our unit happened to recognize me at the medical facility. He was also heading home—injured—and his parents had come to pick him up. When they heard I needed a ride, they insisted on taking me straight to my apartment. On the way, they spoke warmly and offered comfort that I didn't even know I needed. Before I got out of the car, they gave me their phone numbers and told me their home was always open to me. "You're family now," they said. "Come by anytime."

When I finally stepped into my apartment, I dropped my gear and collapsed onto the couch. I didn't move for what felt like half an hour. I just sat there, staring at the floor. My mind was racing, but I felt completely blank. Less than 24 hours earlier, I had been in Gaza. Now I was here. Safe. Still. Silent.

The first thing I did was take a shower. A long, hot shower. I turned the water from cold to warm and let it run over me like I hadn't felt warmth in weeks—because I hadn't. I reached for real soap. I scrubbed my skin. I stood under the steam and let it pour down my face. I didn't want to leave that shower.

It wasn't just about getting clean. It was like I was trying to wash off the war.

Afterward, I called a few close friends. Their voices grounded me. But when I crawled into bed and rested my head on a pillow—a real pillow, not a helmet or bag of clothes—I couldn't hold it together. The tears came fast, quiet, and deep. A blanket. Four walls. Silence. I was safe, but I wasn't whole.

That night, I woke up several times, heart pounding. For a split second, I thought I was still in Gaza. The room was dark, the silence too quiet. My hand instinctively reached to my side—but the machine gun wasn't there. My body was home. My mind was still at war.

A few days later, I was reassigned to a base in Ma'ale Adumim, a city just east of Jerusalem. Physically, I was starting to feel a bit better. The inflammation had gone down, and I had regained some strength. But the sharp pain was still there—especially in the mornings when I'd get out of bed and feel it shoot up my spine like a reminder of what I had carried.

At this new post, I was tasked with guarding the base, this time using a Tavor X95—a compact Israeli rifle that was much lighter and easier to handle than the MAG machine gun. It was still a responsibility, still part of the mission, but it didn't strain my body the same way. It allowed me to stay active without pushing my limits.

Even so, I couldn't shake the sense of restlessness. I was standing still—but my mind kept moving, looping through the past few weeks, trying to make sense of everything I had just lived through.

It was around this time that the Lone Soldier Center called me. They didn't wait—they assigned me immediately to a psychologist. In those first few meetings, I learned something important: I was showing signs of PTSD. Nothing extreme, but enough that I had to acknowledge it. Ever since the moment a drone came frighteningly close above me in Gaza, I found myself turning around constantly if someone walked behind me. My body carried the tension of danger even when it wasn't there. Understanding that helped me realize this wasn't a weakness—it was a natural reaction to what I had lived through.

Soon after, my official release came. I was done with my service.

There's a tradition in Israel when a soldier finishes their time. You take your *choger*—your military ID band—and cut it. A simple act with a powerful meaning: your duty is finished. You're free.

I held the scissors and hesitated. I thought about my unit still inside Gaza. I thought about the friends I had lost.

Then I cut it. And just like that—it was over.

We celebrated. My adoptive family, friends, and fellow lone soldiers threw a small party. We laughed. We ate. We danced. On the outside, it looked like joy. But inside, I felt something else.

Because for them, the war was over.

For me, it wasn't. I carried guilt. Deep guilt. I was home. I was whole.

Others weren't. Some were still out there, risking their lives. Some were in hospitals. Some would never return.

And I couldn't shake the question:

Why me?

But instead of letting that guilt drown me, I decided to do something with it.

I thought back to Argentina, where I had once felt disconnected from my roots, and then deeply reconnected. I reached out to the Jewish communities there. I messaged old friends, synagogues I had visited, and community leaders. I told them I wanted to speak. I didn't have all the answers, but I had my story. And I believed it needed to be told.

To my surprise, the responses came quickly. Invitations, support, and kind words poured in. One anonymous donor from New York reached out after hearing about my plan. He asked for my ID and flight details. Five minutes later, I received a message confirming a round-trip ticket to Buenos Aires. No name. No photo. Just one message:

"Thank you for protecting Am Yisrael. Thank you for speaking your truth."

When I landed in Argentina, I checked into a small Airbnb and tried to calm my nerves. That very night, I gave my first speech.

I stood in front of a room full of strangers. My heart was pounding. But I remembered something I had told myself in Gaza: Breathe. Stand tall. Speak from truth. So I did.

And they listened.

What started as six speeches turned into twelve. Then eighteen. Jewish communities across the country welcomed me into their homes and synagogues. They hosted me for Shabbat. They shared their fears, their hopes, their gratitude. Teenagers came up to me in tears. Some said:

> "I want to join the IDF now."
> "I've never felt this proud to be Jewish."
> "I needed to hear this."

Sometimes I gave three or four speeches in a week. Some nights, I could barely get the words out, especially when I spoke about my fallen friends. In the middle of speaking, my mind would sometimes drift, racing into sudden memories that were hard to control. It was painful, but I reminded myself why I was there: for the communities, for the people who needed to hear the truth. I had to keep it up.

After speeches, I often felt completely drained. To release the stress and recover, I would run. Running became my therapy. Each step on the pavement felt like a release of everything I carried inside—fear, grief, guilt. Running gave me back my balance when my mind and body felt out of control.

I developed a small ritual: right before stepping up, I would snap my fingers once—a reminder to be present. To honor them. To keep going.

Eventually, I was invited to Spain. Another country. Another community. Same mission. Through it all, I realized something powerful:

If I want this journey to last, it can't end with speeches. Speeches are heard and forgotten. But a book can be read again and again.

A book can reach people across oceans, across generations.

A book can sit on a shelf and wait for the right moment—when someone needs it most.

So here it is:

This book is for the lone soldier who wonders if they matter.

For the teenager unsure of their Jewish identity.

For the mother who lights Shabbat candles and prays for peace.

For the one who stayed. For the one who left.

For the one who survived—and the one who didn't.

This story is for us.

Because the mission never really ends.

CHAPTER 14
TO THE NEXT LONE SOLDIER
THERE WILL BE DAYS WHEN EVERYTHING FEELS TOO HEAVY

Your vest will weigh more than just protection—it will carry the names of people you've lost, the hopes of those who love you, and the silent fears you won't know how to speak aloud.

There will be moments when the silence is louder than the gunfire. When you're sitting in the dark with nothing but your breath and your heartbeat, wondering if you made the right choice. If you're strong enough. If you belong here.

Let me tell you now: you do.

You may have come here alone, like I did.
A plane ticket, a packed bag, a quiet promise to serve something greater than yourself.
You may feel like no one back home will ever truly understand what you've done—or why.

But I promise you: you are not alone.

Not in the sleepless nights.
Not in the aching feet or the sand in your teeth or the blisters on your back.
Not in the moments when you miss your family so much it hurts to breathe.
And not in the silent tears you'll wipe away before anyone sees.

TO THE NEXT LONE SOLDIER

You are one in a line of thousands.
Young men and women who came before you, who stood where you now stand.
Who left behind comfort to find meaning.
Who traded ordinary lives for something extraordinary: purpose.

There's a strength in you that you haven't yet met.
It'll show up when the weight gets unbearable—when you think you're done.
It'll rise from your gut and whisper, *"Keep going."*

I've seen it.
I found it in myself, even when I didn't believe it was there.

To the next lone soldier—remember this:

- You're allowed to be afraid.
- You're allowed to question everything.
- You're allowed to break down—and then rise again.

Because strength isn't measured in how much you carry—it's in how much you keep walking, even when everything inside you begs to stop.

Never forget who you are.
Where you come from.
Why you're here.

You're not just protecting a land.
You're protecting memory, identity, history, and hope.

You're protecting every child who deserves to grow up without the sound of sirens. Every grandparent who prayed for peace but never saw it.

Every story that was almost erased—but wasn't.

You carry all of that now.

And one day, when your service is over, and you return to the world that has no idea what you've been through, you'll sit quietly and think of moments no one else will ever know.

They won't see the war behind your eyes.
But they'll see something in you:
A quiet strength.
A fierce compassion.
A kind of peace that was paid for in sleepless nights and unwavering courage.

And maybe—just maybe—you'll write a letter like this one.

So here it is, from me to you:

You're doing better than you think.
You're stronger than you know.
And you are never, ever alone.

With respect,
A lone soldier who once stood where you now stand.

CLOSING WORDS

As I write these final lines, I know there will never be perfect words to capture this journey. What I do know is simple: never be afraid to stand up for what's right and protect what you love.

When I was handed that machine gun for the first time, I didn't know how to carry its weight—physically or mentally. But I learned. I learned that stepping forward, even when you're scared or unsure, is what it means to take responsibility. I wasn't fearless; I was just willing to stand for something bigger than myself.

People say only the craziest soldiers carry the machine gun. Maybe I was a little crazy—or maybe I just believed enough to do what needed to be done. I look back now at those nights in Gaza, the fear, the small moments of courage—and I still don't fully understand how I did it. But I do know I didn't do it alone.

The strength to carry on came from my family, my friends, my brothers beside me, and the unshakable belief that Am Yisrael, the people of Israel, are worth protecting.

I hope that if you remember anything from my story, it's this: when the moment comes, pick up what you have—your hands, your words, your heart—and stand up for what's right. No matter how heavy it feels, you're never alone.

Thank you for walking this road with me. Thank you for listening, for caring, and for remembering. May we always have the courage to protect, to stand together, and to live for those who can't.

Am Yisrael Chai. The people of Israel live.

ACKNOWLEDGMENTS

Writing this book has been one of the most meaningful journeys of my life, and it wouldn't have been possible without the incredible people who supported me along the way.

To my parents, thank you for giving me the strength to pursue this path. Your sacrifices and unwavering belief in me have been my foundation.

To my brothers and sisters, you have always been my greatest support system, reminding me that no matter where I am, family is my anchor.

To Libbie Snyder, thank you for guiding me through this entire process—from the very first page to the final word. Your encouragement and wisdom made this book possible.

To the Yavin family, thank you for giving me a home in Israel and showing me the true meaning of an adopted family. Your kindness and warmth will always have a special place in my heart.

To the Bayit Brigade and Growing Wings, thank you for giving me a true home and always supporting my path. Your constant encouragement, open arms, and belief in me made all the difference, both in the creation of this book and throughout my journey as a lone soldier.

To David Mittan, thank you for all the support you've given me, especially during my travels to Spain for hasbara. Your encouragement has meant so much along this journey.

To my fellow soldiers, thank you for teaching me the meaning of resilience, courage, and brotherhood. Together, we endured challenges that tested every part of us, and I will carry those memories with me forever.

To the Michael Levin Base, a lone soldier center that has stood by me from the very beginning of my service up until today. Your endless support, guidance, and community have carried me through every stage, and I am deeply grateful.

To Nathanel Young Z"L, your spirit continues to inspire me. The quote you loved, "Some people want it to happen, some wish it could happen, others make it happen," will forever remind me to strive for action over hesitation.

And finally, to you, the reader, thank you for allowing me to share this journey with you. It's my hope that these pages reflect not only my story but the strength, love, and unity that make us all resilient.

www.ingramcontent.com/pod-product-compliance
Lightning Source LLC
Chambersburg PA
CBHW060604080526
44585CB00013B/682